The Blended Family Activity Book

THE BLENDED FAMILY ACTIVITY BOOK

75 Fun Activities to Help Families Connect and Spend Time Together

Julie Johnson, M.Ed.

ROCKRIDGE
PRESS

Interior and Cover Designer: Erik Jacobsen
Art Producer: Tom Hood
Editor: Mo Mozuch
Production Manager: Jose Olivera

All illustrations used under license from iStock. Author photo courtesy of Shelly Hamalian.

Paperback ISBN: 978-1-63807-358-1
eBook ISBN: 978-1-63878-008-3
R0

To Octavio, for helping
dreams come true.

CONTENTS

INTRODUCTION

A few days after my son was born, my five-year-old stepdaughter carefully and quietly carried him in his bouncy chair to a room in the back of the house that wasn't used much. When I walked back into the living room and found him missing, she said, "He has gone to the baby dungeon, and that's where he should stay!"

This year, she turned 17 and her brother turned 12. Nowadays, they walk to the farmers' market together on Saturday mornings to buy fresh-baked croissants and apple juice, and some nights they cuddle in bed together and read.

It wasn't always like that, though. The early years of our blended family were hard. The spark my stepdaughter had before my son was born seemed to dim after his birth. Her tantrums could taint a whole afternoon, and her refusals were set in stone. One evening, after a long day of exhausting power struggles with her, I asked my partner what we should do. He looked at me, weary and exhausted, and said, "survive." Although the early years felt like survival, we eventually began to thrive.

After being in education for many years, working in schools and nonprofits, I became a parent coach and learned tools that changed our family dynamic. Many of the activities in this book were an important part of what we did as a family to nurture individual relationships and build our family as a whole.

While these activities will help you work through the challenges in a blended family, if you're experiencing serious and ongoing debilitating feelings, please reach out to a medical or mental health professional.

It takes time for a family to blend. The journey will have its bright spots. But it will also have its days when the light ahead looks dim. Trying to be one big happy family in the beginning can be difficult, and some days, futile. But with trust and patience, it's possible.

The activities in this book will support the process as you continue to navigate the different dynamics of your family.

Blending a family, where one or both parents have one or more children from a previous relationship, can bring up big feelings for everyone. Grief, anger, resentment, and jealousy are not uncommon experiences in blended families. For some members, there has been the loss of a previous family configuration, and for some children and stepparents, anger, jealousy, and resentment are brewing under the surface.

This book will help alleviate some of the challenges of blended families through creativity, connection, movement, and mindfulness. It will help you find common ground where you thought there was none. And it will help build the safety and trust that is so needed in a blended family—whether it is one that is struggling to adjust or one that wants to come together to build connection and have fun.

If you are in the beginning stages of blending a family or even several years in and the road still seems long and arduous, there is hope. Children are resilient and things can change. The fact that you're willing to dip your toes in, try some new activities, reflect on some of the challenges, and create even more meaningful connections in your family says a lot about you and your family. I can't wait for you to explore the pages ahead. Let's get started!

HOW TO USE THIS BOOK

This book consists of 75 off-page activities for blended families to do together. It is divided into 15 chapters, and each chapter has a different theme. While there are opportunities for families to bond through art and music in chapter 1, in chapter 2 there are suggestions for family conversations, both serious and fun. By exploring one's experience in a blended family, or problem-solving an issue together, family members can practice effective communication as they develop trust and safety in a new configuration.

Chapter 3 helps family members take their mind away from conflict and tension by going on a mindful walk, creating a special space in the home where all members of the family can find a peaceful retreat, and carving out time for gratitude.

Chapter 4 consists of activities that expand a family's imagination, tapping into each person's creativity and ability to see things differently. Chapter 5 invites families to get adventurous, whereas chapter 6 and chapter 7 help families explore the past and the future.

Chapter 8 consists of activities that test everyone's brainpower, and chapter 9 and chapter 11 will get you moving. While chapter 10 and chapter 12 help the family build trust, chapter 13 and chapter 14 focus on relationships, and chapter 15 brings your family together through the power of technology.

You may want to make some activities a weekly ritual, whereas others can be done when the mood is right. You may tackle multiple activities at once or bring out the book on a family vacation or even a long road trip.

While some activities may bring up touchy topics, others will help you handle the stress of a blended family. Many of the activities are intended to increase mutual respect and some may induce laughter. All the activities will nurture the relationships in your family and help each person thrive.

CHAPTER ONE

Get Creative

Through music, art, and creative expression, the activities in this chapter will help a blended family build community, celebrate each person's uniqueness, and create a positive vision for the year ahead. While Musical Telephone (page 2) can bring playfulness and laughter to a tense family dynamic, The Family Portrait (page 3) helps each person feel they have a place in the family as they navigate a new family structure. There is also the opportunity to grow new roots and collaborate by making a DIY Terrarium (page 5). By creating A Family Vision Board (page 7), everyone realizes that even if some decisions about the family are out of their hands, they can decide how they want to feel and the experiences they want to have in the months and even years ahead.

Musical Telephone

If you like the traditional game of telephone, you'll love the musical version. Musical Telephone requires careful listening as each person tries to imitate the sounds that have been made by their family members. In this activity, a blended family is creating a universal language that can unite people across differences and build community. In the process, Musical Telephone will create lots of laughter!

INSTRUCTIONS

1. Decide who will go first.

2. The first person makes a sound using their body. They can tap a beat on their chest, clap their hands in a rhythmic pattern, stomp their feet, or even make the sound of a bird or other animal.

3. The second person imitates the sound of the first person and comes up with a sound of their own.

4. The third person repeats the sounds of the first two people and offers an additional unique sound to the family song.

5. Continue in this way until each person has had the chance to repeat the previous sounds in the correct order and add their own.

6. At the end, you'll have a medley of different sounds that each family member has contributed to—and remembered!

Let's Talk About It: Music is a great way to bring together people of different ages and interests, and it can even lead to lots of laughter. Was it more or less fun than a traditional game of telephone? What did you find challenging about this activity? What was the funniest moment of the activity?

For Next Time: Another fun way to do Musical Telephone is to use musical instruments or noisemakers. If you don't have any instruments on hand, use pots and pans or a ruler and a plastic container to create a family song.

The Family Portrait

This is a fun activity that gets everyone's creative juices flowing. It's a good way to learn about one another in a new blended family—an opportunity to appreciate one another's skills and qualities and discover what each person loves.

SUPPLIES

- Tape
- Paper
- Light

- Assorted pens, colored pencils, and markers
- Paints and watercolors (optional)

INSTRUCTIONS

1. Tape a large piece of paper to the wall at the height of your head and shoulders.

2. Move a light close enough to cast a shadow of you onto the paper.

3. Turn sideways so that a shadow of your profile appears on the paper.

4. Have a partner trace the outline of your head and upper body.

5. Fill in the silhouette with words, symbols, or pictures.

6. Focus on positive traits and attributes. Each family member should fill in their silhouette with what makes them unique and special. Things to consider include:

- What do you like about yourself?
- What skills do you have?

- What are your favorite things to do?
- What do you love?

Continued »

The Family Portrait continued

7. When each person is finished filling in their silhouette, find a place to hang them. You can create a family portrait by putting everyone together.

Let's Talk About It: This activity can help blended family members put aside any resentment or jealousies as each person focuses on what they appreciate about themselves and notice what they like about their family. As you created your silhouette, what did you learn about yourself? What did you learn about one another? What's something that surprised you about someone in your family?

For Next Time: Try adding keepsakes—small objects you have around the home that represent something you love. Young children can create images, while older children can use words and symbols to depict their thoughts, hopes, and dreams. Some people may want to use watercolors or paints instead of markers or colored pencils.

DIY Terrarium

Bring the rain forest to you. For blended families, a planting project is a great creative outlet, and, for children who go from one house to another, it symbolizes stability and belonging. Terraria are easier to maintain than outside gardens and even some house-plants. In this activity, you'll design an open terrarium. You may choose to do one larger terrarium for the whole family or smaller individual ones.

SUPPLIES

- Glass jar, vase, old fish tank, goldfish bowl, or see-through plastic container
- Gravel or small pebbles
- Activated charcoal (optional)
- Potting soil
- Plants that work well in open terraria, such as succulents, cacti, and aloe
- Branches, rocks, and/or seashells (optional)
- Spray bottle

INSTRUCTIONS

1. Come together with your family and decide what kind of container to use and what kinds of plants to purchase. If you already have small succulents around the house or in your yard, you may want to start with those.

2. When it comes to choosing a container for your terrarium, anything from an old pickle jar to an unused fish tank will work.

3. The best plants for an open terrarium are succulents, air plants, and cacti—anything that can thrive without consistent humidity and moisture. Other good choices include zebra plants, mother of pearl, flapjacks, and earth stars.

4. Add a layer of gravel or small pebbles to your chosen container. You may also want to add a thin layer of activated charcoal to prevent bacteria and odor from developing in the container. However, charcoal is not essential for open terraria.

Continued »

5. You'll then add 2 to 3 inches of moist potting soil and place your plants in the terrarium. You can complete the look with an optional layer of decorative pebbles

6. You can get creative by decorating the terrarium with other elements, such as bark, twigs, rocks, or shells. Terraria offer a fun opportunity to express your creativity.

7. Be careful not to overstuff the container, as you'll need room for new growth.

8. Find a location in your home that will provide sufficient light, and place the terrarium there.

9. You will want to water the terrarium regularly depending on the watering requirements for the plants you've chosen. Generally, once every 10 days or 2 weeks.

10. Over time, as things grow, you'll need to prune your plants as well.

Let's Talk About It: Making decisions together as a blended family is important. When family members know that they have a say in a project, it helps them feel valued. What was your favorite part about planning and creating a terrarium with your family? What did you learn about plants during this project? What would you add to your terrarium next time?

For Next Time: There are lots of fun variations to try in the future. Find a hanging vase and put your open terrarium in a window or bright spot of the room. You can also use old spice jars to make mini terraria. Younger children may want to add small plastic animals or fairies to their terraria. You can also use colored sand to make a desert terrarium.

A Family Vision Board

A Family Vision Board is a great way for each family member to feel hopeful about the future. In some blended families, children feel powerless or resentful about the decisions that have been made. Whether it's how much time they see each parent, or simply that the biological parents are not together anymore, a vision board helps every member of the family learn that they can eventually create the kind of life they want, even if they've experienced loss or disappointment. Creating a vision board helps each person feel hopeful and empowered.

SUPPLIES

- Paper
- Assorted pens, colored pencils, and markers
- Cardboard, stock paper, poster board, or corkboard
- Magazines
- Scissors
- Glue or tape
- Thumbtacks (if using a corkboard)

INSTRUCTIONS

1. Begin this activity by exploring what each member of the family wants to achieve in the coming year (or more). Identify one person to jot down notes on paper as each person shares their thoughts. Some questions that can help spur a conversation or a writing exercise include:

- What's something we've done in the past as a family and would like to do again?
- How do you picture an ideal afternoon, weekend, or holiday together?
- What makes you happy or feel good?
- What do you want more of in the coming year?
- Are there any places you want to visit?
- What new skills would you like to learn or what is something you could get better at?

Continued »

2. Once you've brainstormed some ideas, you can divide up tasks so that each person looks for images that represent a specific vision on your board.

3. Gather pictures and words from magazines that represent your vision. You can even be green and go through your junk mail for material, too. If you've talked about wanting things like more laughter or downtime together, you can write words or draw symbols that represent those feelings and actions as well.

4. Decide as a team how you want your goals and desires arranged on the board, and glue or tape them to create a collage of dreams. If you're using a corkboard, you can simply attach pictures with thumbtacks.

5. When the vision board is complete, hang it in a place where everyone can see it. This may be on a living room mantel, the refrigerator, or a dining room wall.

Let's Talk About It: This activity allows every family member to express what they want for their family and can be used as a time to create new traditions or rituals to help a blended family feel more cohesive. What were the similarities and differences you noticed in what each person wanted? Notice what you already have in your life and express gratitude for those things that are already present and those things you'd like to see more of.

For Next Time: This activity makes a great family tradition at any time of the year. If possible, have magazines that appeal to all family members, including kid's magazines for younger children. You can also leave space on the vision board to add images, words, and symbols throughout the year. A year after the vision board has been created—or any time of the year for that matter—you can reflect as a family on what has come to fruition and what you are still working toward.

A Family Found Poem

Create a literary collage with A Family Found Poem. Found poems are a fun and creative way for family members to expand on a common theme, object, or idea. It's a great way for blended families with different interests and personalities to find common ground so that each person feels more connected to the family as a whole. Through this activity, you can enjoy a recent memory or expand on an object or idea that everyone likes.

SUPPLIES

- Paper
- Assorted pens, colored pencils, and markers
- Newspapers
- Magazines
- Printouts of poems
- Poetry books or children's books
- Scissors
- Glue

INSTRUCTIONS

1. Find a space where everyone can work together. It could be a large table, a desk, or the floor.

2. Choose a theme or big idea that you want the poem to be about. It might be something everyone in the family is fond of, like golden retrievers or jelly donuts. Or it could be a memory the whole family shares (for example, last year at the lake), or a big idea like love or laughter.

3. Spread out newspapers, magazines, photocopies of pages from poetry, or picture books, and even junk mail.

4. Start choosing your words. Each person looks through the material to find words and phrases they like. Look for words that help you visualize the theme of your poem. Once you've landed on words and phrases you like, start cutting.

Continued »

A Family Found Poem continued

5. When each person is satisfied with the words and phrases they've found, spread them out so that you can see all the clippings. The whole family will then have to decide the format of the poem.

6. Try moving the words around into different configurations. Questions to consider include:

- Do you want stanzas?

- Can you create similes or metaphors with the words you have?

- Do you want your poem to rhyme?

- How about repetition?

7. Don't forget to add a title. Discuss these literary elements.

8. When you've agreed on how you want your poem to look, have everyone work together to start pasting.

9. When completed, hang your poem in a place where everyone can see it.

Let's Talk About It: The found poem is a wonderful way to celebrate similarities and differences in a blended family. How easy or difficult was it to land on a theme that everyone liked? What did you notice about one another's preferences? If you chose a family memory, like a recent excursion, how did each person's account of the experience differ? What are some other materials or texts you can use for your found poems?

For Next Time: Found poems are also a great way to dive deeper into a text and develop a new understanding of it. With younger children, you can read a picture book aloud and then create a found poem from words and phrases in the book. Older children may have fun creating a found poem from a novel they are reading. If each person creates their own poem, don't forget to celebrate. You may want to follow dinner with a special dessert and poetry reading.

Spark Conversation

Good communication is an essential element of success in a blended family. Without it, stepparents can feel underappreciated in a blended family, and children can feel like there is less time and attention for them when a parent has remarried or they've acquired new siblings. In this chapter, you'll find activities that help your family members listen, share their thoughts, decrease roadblocks to communication, and develop mutual understanding and appreciation. While some activities focus on appreciation, others invite family members to find common ground. When these practices are woven into the family culture, it builds trust, understanding, and a positive mind-set.

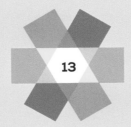

Communication Origami

Kick-start a good conversation with a few folds of paper. This activity helps you see how information can be interpreted in different ways by different people.

SUPPLIES

- Paper

- Origami instructions from a book or the internet (optional)

INSTRUCTIONS

1. Choose one person in the family who would like to be the first to give directions.

2. Give everyone else one sheet of paper and instruct them to close their eyes.

3. Have the person leading the activity fold a piece of paper using the directions in step 4. They will then give the other family members instructions on how to fold and tear the paper to create a shape.

4. Those who are doing the folding should keep their eyes closed and are not allowed to ask questions. For example, you can use these instructions to create a geometric shape with paper.

   a. Begin by folding your piece of paper in half.

   b. Tear off the upper right-hand corner.

   c. Fold your paper in half again.

   d. Tear off the lower right-hand corner.

   e. Fold your paper in half.

   f. Tear off the upper left-hand corner.

   g. Fold your paper in half again.

   h. Tear off the lower left-hand corner.

   i. Unfold your paper and hold it up.

CHAPTER TWO

5. Once everyone is done, they can compare shapes and see the differences.

Let's Talk About It: **Communication can be interpreted differently by different people. Were you tempted to look at what other people were doing? What can these frustrations teach us about communicating? Did you notice any differences in temperament among the family? Some people might've leaned in and had fun, others may have felt embarrassed or angry. This can give you useful insight for resolving conflicts in the future.**

For Next Time: **In another version of this activity, each person starts out with one sheet of paper and follows the first direction. Then each person passes their paper to the person sitting next to them until all the folds are done. This modification is great for any family members who may be hearing impaired. Also, using blindfolds can make this more fun (and more honest) for younger kids in the family.**

Name That Emotion

Blended families evoke many emotions, from sadness and grief to the joy of discovery and the excitement of new relationships. This is a great way to learn how each person in the family expresses their feelings through body language and gestures and can reduce moments of misunderstanding.

SUPPLIES

- Assorted pens, colored pencils, and markers
- Index cards or small pieces of paper

INSTRUCTIONS

1. Have the whole family print emotion words on index cards or small slips of paper. Use words such as "happy," "scared," "sad," "angry," "satisfied," "worried," "annoyed," "nervous," and "loving."

2. Place the cards into a pile or container and mix them up.

3. Begin by identifying one person to pick out a card (without showing the others) and acting out the emotion that is printed on the card.

4. When acting out what is on the card, the person can use only facial expressions, gestures, and other body language—no words.

5. The other family members try to guess the emotion.

6. Whoever guesses the emotion correctly takes a turn by drawing a new card.

Let's Talk About It: Sometimes you're not even aware of the message your face is sending. Were some emotions easier to guess than others? Why? What did you notice about how people expressed emotions? Did you learn something new about someone in your family?

For Next Time: Another variation of this activity is for the player to draw a card and give verbal clues instead of acting out the emotion. For example, someone draws a card that says "frustrated" and then tells the rest of the family, "You might feel this way when someone eats the last scoop of ice cream."

The Family Meeting

The Family Meeting is a time when both children and adults can learn the art of problem-solving and create a space to appreciate one another, even when things are tense. This activity is great for a blended family because it helps everyone feel like they have a say in how the family is run by getting to share their appreciations and suggestions.

INSTRUCTIONS

1. Decide on a good time for everyone to come together. If you can make it a regular weekly or bimonthly event, that is even better.

2. In the first meeting, you'll want to come up with ground rules together so that everyone feels like they can share, listen, and reflect in a safe space. Examples of ground rules include:

   Everyone has the chance to share.

   One person talks at a time.

   Be kind—no putdowns or ouches.

   Respect other people's opinions even if you don't agree.

3. After stating the ground rules, the first item on the agenda should be appreciations. When each person appreciates someone else, it sets a positive tone for the meeting. Adults may want to model appreciating each person first: "I appreciated building that fort with Ella this week. It was a lot of fun." "I appreciated the delicious dinner that Bill made the other night when I had to work late."

4. The next part of the meeting—which is the bulk of it—will focus on likes and suggestions for change. Have each person share one thing that's going well in the family and one thing they would like changed or done differently. Even though the parents still make the rules, children should have the opportunity to make suggestions that the parents can consider.

Continued »

5. A child may want to discuss a trip to Disneyland or more time on technology, whereas a parent may want to talk about getting to bed on time with less dawdling. Even though you may not be able to go to Disneyland, you can brainstorm fun things that you can do together.

6. This is not the time to talk to one child about changing their behavior, but it is a good time, for example, to brainstorm solutions for getting chores done on a regular basis, or to decide who will walk the dog and when.

7. When conflict arises, you'll want to acknowledge each person's needs and desires while brainstorming solutions.

8. Close the meeting by having each person say something they are looking forward to.

Let's Talk About It: **Having a conversation about the structure of the meeting is a great way to get buy-in from each family member. What did you like about The Family Meeting? What would you do differently? Do you think one person should facilitate the meeting each time or should we rotate facilitators next time?**

For Next Time: **Keep a family notebook during meetings so that you can record family agreements that are made during discussions. You can refer back to these agreements during future meetings and revise them if necessary. If your children are very young, keep the meeting focused on appreciations—what they like about your family and what they want to do more of.**

Conversation Starters

Each child in a blended family has a unique experience, and yet most children share the common experience of loss—the loss of a family unit they once knew. They have thoughts, feelings, and opinions about their blended family that are important to hear. When you put time into understanding what the blended family experience is like for each person, it opens up a path to trust, healing, and hope.

INSTRUCTIONS

Here are some conversation starters that will help strengthen the communication in your family. Some days a formal setting, like The Family Meeting (page 17), may be appropriate to ask them. And sometimes a conversation will arise organically when both children and adults feel relaxed and connected. Some questions in this activity are more serious than others. Some days you may choose the lighter questions for fun.

QUESTIONS

1. How are blended families different from traditional families?

2. Do any of your friends or other people you know live in blended families?

3. When you grow up, do you think you and your siblings and stepsiblings will stay connected?

4. Are you able to tell me or others when something is upsetting you?

5. When you're sad, what makes you feel better?

6. What do you think are some of your best qualities?

7. What's a time when you felt brave?

8. What's something about you that I may not know?

Continued »

9. If you wrote a book, what would it be about?

10. What is the best part of getting older?

11. What are you least looking forward to about getting older?

12. What's your biggest dream?

13. What time of day do you like best—morning, noon, or night?

14. What makes you laugh?

15. What does a perfect day look like for you? What makes it special?

16. What are your superpowers?

17. What do you love about your friends?

18. If you could choose a different name, what would it be?

19. What's one place you hope to travel to one day?

20. How would you change the world if you could?

Let's Talk About It: Asking the right questions helps a child feel heard. When a parent inquires in a warm and welcoming way, without a particular agenda or concern, and listens without interrupting, a child can feel safe and seen. Afterward, you may want to ask your kids, are these questions hard to answer, or are they helpful?

For Next Time: Another way to do this activity is to guess how someone in the family will answer the question. For example, someone can ask a family member, "What do you think Diana's favorite food is?" The lighter questions can be used in long car rides. You can also have children come up with their own questions.

The Family Wheel

Sometimes interests aren't shared by everyone in the blended family. Dad and his daughters may have a love of in-line skating, but stepmom is a beginner. In blended families, often someone feels like an outsider, and it can be difficult to notice what family members have in common. Noticing the commonalities each person shares in this activity can reduce the feeling of isolation as an outsider and can be a jumping-off point for a low-stress activity together. Taking time to appreciate each person's unique differences can help everyone feel like they hold a special place in the family.

SUPPLIES

- Assorted pens, colored pencils, and markers
- Paper (any size paper will do, but larger is better)

INSTRUCTIONS

1. Identify one family member to draw a large wheel on the selected paper by drawing a circle in the middle and lines (or spokes) extending out from the center of the circle.

2. Have the group brainstorm five things that they all have in common. Write those things in the center of the wheel. Things to consider include: where each person was born, what sport or activity they love, what hobbies they enjoy, and what fun qualities they have.

3. Then find one thing about each person that is different and unique—something that no one else shares. Maybe it is a hobby or favorite food. Does someone love sleeping out underneath the stars, while someone else likes glamping? Write each person's unique quality or interest on the spokes surrounding the circle.

4. Once the wheel is completed, take time to have each person say more about their unique quality or interest. If someone likes sleeping out underneath the stars, what do they enjoy most about that experience? Where was their favorite place to sleep outside? Where is a new place they would like to explore?

Continued »

The Family Wheel continued

Let's Talk About It: It is important to appreciate ways that family members are different, but it is equally important to notice what you have in common. Doing so will help you feel closer, lessening the outsider experience for some family members. What does everyone in the family have in common? What are your differences? What surprised you about your similarities and differences?

For Next Time: To add to this activity, you can make more circles around the original one. Each circle can have a theme such as sports that everyone likes, foods that the whole family enjoys, or activities that you like to do on the weekend. An additional way to learn about one another is to give each person a different-colored marker and have them circle the activities they'd enjoy. This can be used to plan your next family outing. Another way to look at similarities and differences is to write a number from 1 to 10 on index cards or pieces of paper. Put them in a line in numerical order on the wall or on the floor. Have family members come up with a list of items such as soccer, mint chip ice cream, and bike riding. As you go through the list of items, each person moves to the number that best represents how they feel about it. One means you hate it and 10 means you love it.

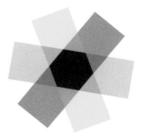

Be Mindful

Often in blended families the focus is on problem-solving, which means putting a lot of our energy into looking at the negative. This can take a toll on the whole family. The activities in this chapter are designed to aid a shift to positive thinking. It helps blended families notice what they enjoy about one another and about themselves, which can alleviate all-too-common feelings of sadness, anger, or resentment. These activities strengthen individual relationships in the family through appreciation and gratitude, and they increase each person's ability to self-reflect, focus, and relax—qualities that help you navigate the challenges in blended families.

The Flower of Appreciation

Sometimes stepchildren and stepparents have trouble seeing what they like in one another. Making time to notice and appreciate everyone's qualities can help family members build trust and other positive feelings.

SUPPLIES

- Paper
- Assorted pens, colored pencils, and markers

INSTRUCTIONS

1. Find a comfortable place to sit and give each person a piece of paper.

2. Instruct each person to write their name in the middle of the paper, then draw a circle around it. The circle will be used as the center of the flower.

3. Draw large petals around the circle that is being used as the center of the flower. Make sure that each petal has enough space to write a few words within it.

4. There should be at least one petal for each member of the family.

5. Pass the flowers around so that everyone can write something they appreciate about the person in the petals of their flower.

6. At the end of the activity, find a place to hang the flowers in your home.

Let's Talk About It: **Appreciation helps both children and adults be more cooperative, creative, and caring toward others. Which qualities do you have in common with other family members? What are your favorite qualities about yourself?**

For Next Time: **Think about how to make appreciation a regular part of your family culture. If dinnertime is a source of stress, spend time before or during the meal appreciating each person.**

Noticing Nature

Getting out into nature can help reduce depression and anxiety—experiences that are not uncommon for stepparents. Adding the elements of mindfulness and journaling to a nature walk can improve your mood and help reduce tension and anxiety in the family.

SUPPLIES

- A small container or envelope for each person
- Assorted pens, colored pencils, and markers
- Notebooks or journals

INSTRUCTIONS

1. Gather your family and tell them you're heading out for a nature walk.

2. Make sure each person has a small container to collect items in—interesting rocks, leaves, shells, or acorns. A small bag or envelope works. And make sure each child has something to write with and a journal or something else to write in.

3. Notice what you see, hear, feel, and smell as you begin your walk. Do you hear birds or sirens, or is there silence? Maybe the smell of bluebells or pine needles strikes you. As you pick up items in nature to observe, how do they feel?

4. Find a place to sit and take out your notebooks or journals. Older children may want to both write and draw about what they see, while younger children can illustrate their environment. A writing or illustration prompt can simply be: "What do you see, hear, feel, and smell?" You can modify this for any family members who may have vision or hearing impairments.

5. As you write and draw, you can add found objects to the pages of your journal.

Continued »

Noticing Nature continued

Let's Talk About It: Changing your awareness of something you do on a regular basis—by bringing your senses and creativity to it—can change your whole perspective and give you new insights. Can you think of another place to bring your journal that would be fun? Did you find anything special outside? What was the hardest thing about this activity? What would make it easier next time?

For Next Time: Make it a regular, fun outing to visit other places with your notepad—like parks, nature reserves, lakes, and beaches. Find books to help you identify the plants and birds you see. There are even apps, such as PlantSnap, to help you identify the flora.

You can find more meaningful ways to interact with your environments as well. Take some trashbags with you and clean up things along the way. Or you can research some safe-to-eat plants or mushrooms and try your hand at foraging!

The Calming Glitter Jar

Mix glitter, glue, and water for the perfect storm. Making a calming glitter jar is a fun family project that teaches everyone about emotions and mindfulness. When emotions are running high, glitter jars are a good way to bring mindfulness to the moment and shift your attention away from the upset. If a conversation gets heated, you can take a break, shake the jar, and wait for the glitter to settle before resuming the conversation.

SUPPLIES

- Glass or plastic containers with screw-top lids, like a mason jar or plastic water bottle
- Distilled water
- ½ cup glitter glue or clear glue
- 1 to 2 tablespoons glitter
- Food coloring (optional)

INSTRUCTIONS

1. Come together with the family and explain to younger kids that sometimes we have big feelings that feel like a storm inside of us.

2. When you are angry, sad, or nervous, and need something soothing to settle your feelings, you can take a mindfulness break.

3. As you shake a glitter jar, it erupts into a flurry of sparkles—similar to the storm that's brewing in you. But as you watch it settle and breathe calmly as the glitter floats to the bottom of the jar, you're helping soothe any upset that's making it hard to think clearly. This is great for adults, too!

HERE'S HOW TO MAKE A CALMING GLITTER JAR

1. Fill your jar or plastic bottle with ½ cup of distilled water.

2. Add ½ cup of glitter glue or clear glue to the jar. Keep in mind that the more glue you use, the longer it will take for the glitter to settle after you've shaken it.

3. Add 1 to 2 tablespoons of glitter. You can add different types of glitter, for example, both small and large specks, for a fun design.

Continued »

4. If you're using food coloring, add it now. Experiment with different colors that complement or contrast your glitter.

5. Fill the jar the rest of the way with water and screw the lid on tight. Seal the lid with glue. If you have a glue gun, this makes it easier. If not, simply spread glue around the rim of the jar or plastic bottle and seal.

Let's Talk About It: Glitter jars can be used as a mindfulness tool for the whole family. When you shake the jar, you see a flurry of glitter. We can compare that to when we're upset and flooded with emotion. It's hard to think clearly in those moments when we feel like we're about to explode or our emotions are already running high. But when you breathe through it and take a break with the glitter jar, it helps both your body and mind rest and relax. What did you enjoy about making a glitter jar? What are some creative ways you can use it?

For Next Time: Try adding a small squirt of liquid soap or baby oil for a slower-moving "galaxy" effect. Glitter jars can be used as timers as well. Shake the jar and by the time the glitter settles, everyone, including parents, has to have their pajamas on. A family race to put pajamas on (let the little kids win, of course!) is a fun way to get ready for bed and often gets the giggles going.

Gratitude Time

Make time for gratitude! Research on gratitude supports an association between gratitude, happiness, and optimism. In a blended family, gratitude can help remedy growing resentment and strengthen family bonds. A regular practice of gratitude enhances empathy and helps people feel closer and more connected. Expressing gratitude for other people on a regular basis can help you feel better about yourself, which means you may fare better during transitions or other challenging times. There are many ways to express gratitude. You can be thankful for events or people in your past, and you can express gratitude for the present. You can even be thankful for the future as you express gratitude for what you're looking forward to. This is a powerful way to shape what's yet to come.

SUPPLIES

- Assorted pens, colored pencils, or markers
- Paper
- Jar, container, or envelope to hold small pieces of paper
- Art supplies to decorate the container (optional)

INSTRUCTIONS

1. Choose a regular time of the day or week when family members can come together and share gratitude. Some families find that before bed is a good time to express their gratitude. For other families, dinnertime works best, or during a weekly family meeting.

2. Have each family member write down on a piece of paper what they are grateful for. It can be a small thing. Very young children can share their gratitude aloud and the adults can write it down for them, or a child can draw a picture of what they are grateful for.

Continued »

3. Share a sentence starter with your family: "I am thankful for _____, because _____."

4. Fill the jar, container, or envelope with your family's gratitude statements.

5. Repeat step 3 with other sentence starters, or by giving family members the opportunity to add multiple pieces of paper reflecting things that they are grateful for.

6. When everyone has had time to submit the things they are grateful for, have each person pull a piece of paper from the jar and read the gratitude statement written on it. For young children, have them choose a slip of paper and then have an older sibling or parent read it.

7. The jar can be kept in a place in the home where everyone can see it and contribute to it during the week. You can read from it periodically or create a ritual of reading gratitude statements at a certain time or occasion.

Let's Talk About It: Gratitude can improve your mood quickly and it helps you have a better outlook over time. This is a great practice to incorporate into your daily routine. What do you notice when you express gratitude for people and things in your life? What's something that someone wrote that you would agree with?

For Next Time: Another version of this activity is to share three good things with one another before bed, or a bright spot from the day. You can also try having a gratitude board in a common room where you pin your gratitude statements. Some members of the family may enjoy keeping a gratitude journal, while others might enjoy writing a thank-you note to someone else in the family. Thank-you letters are a great opportunity to express your appreciation for someone and the impact they've had on your life.

A Special Place

Transform a small space in your home where each person can rest and relax. For parents and stepparents, a place to retreat and find calm is important. Some children may need a respite from a busy home with multiple stepsiblings. A designated place to meditate and breathe or relax and read can be a welcome addition in any home, but for blended families it can help repair frayed connections and strengthen the family unit. The mindfulness space should not be used as a place for punishment or time-outs, but rather a quiet space to rest and find solace from the storm.

INSTRUCTIONS

1. Come together with your family and let them know you'd like to create a mindfulness space in your home. This is a good topic for a family meeting or after dinner.

2. The adults may choose to decide where the space is. The special place could be a small portion of the living room, a corner of a study, a closet, a bench in the garden, or even a room of its own.

3. Discuss with your family what the special place will be used for. Some family members may want to use it as a meditation space, while others may find it a peaceful place to read, write, or draw. Emphasize that it should be a quiet space to practice mindfulness—a time to deepen awareness through breath or creativity.

4. You may even mention that parents can use this space when they are mad to breathe through their tension and find calm.

5. Decide how you will decorate the space. You may want to decorate it with throw pillows, a plant, a small rug, or an object that is meaningful to each person in the family. It should be kept clean and uncluttered.

Continued »

A Special Place continued

Let's Talk About It: Give each person a chance to try out the special space. Come together with the family after a week or so and reflect on how you're using it. Does this space help you relax? What special object could you bring to this space so that it represents each person in the family? Are there any challenges or conflicts that have arisen in the space—such as young siblings not being willing to share art supplies or toys? This is a good opportunity to bring siblings together to solve problems. Have children come up with solutions to any conflicts that arise in the space. What would make the special space better?

For Next Time: Bringing nature into the space can have a calming effect. This may mean decorating the space with some flowers you find in your yard or a small plant. You might also try a family meditation in the special space if it's big enough for each person to sit or lie down. You can play soft music or a recorded meditation to help everyone relax. You may also want to find a place in the mindfulness space to hang gratitude cards or appreciations that everyone has written. And you can even take a small object from the space with you when you travel. For young children, it can be comforting to bring a small slice of the special space with you to ease a transition or find comfort in a new place.

CHAPTER FOUR

Use Your Imagination

Your imagination helps you solve problems, develop empathy, and improve your social skills. For blended families, the ability to step into someone else's shoes helps develop empathy and understanding, which are important for establishing new relationships. The activities in this chapter invite families to work together to imagine new environments, new ways of working and creating together, and even new ways of being in the world. They also result in a lot of laughter, something every family needs to help reduce tensions and keep conflicts to a minimum.

Cross the Circle

For blended families, this activity calls on your imagination and creativity and creates new ways to laugh together as you dance or trudge across the room. It provides families with a respite from conflicts as you release tension and giggle together.

INSTRUCTIONS

1. Have your family sit in or create a circle.

2. Identify a leader to kick off the fun.

3. The leader assigns each person either the number one or number two. If the group has more than six people, you may want to assign three numbers.

4. The leader calls a number and instructs that number to walk in a certain way. For example, "Number ones, cross the circle as a ballerina onstage." Everyone who is a one dances across the circle.

5. Each person takes a turn as the leader and gives instructions.

6. Here are some ways to cross the circle. Have fun coming up with your own!

   A ballerina onstage.

   A Siberian tiger in the snow.

   A deer stuck in mud.

   A dog walking on thin ice.

Let's Talk About It: **This activity gets everyone moving in interesting ways. What were your favorite ways of moving? What did you find challenging? What are other ways you could Cross the Circle next time?**

For Next Time: **If the children in your family are younger, think of as many animals as you can and have fun walking like giraffes, birds, or elephants across the circle.**

What's in That Box?

This activity can help move you away from everyday communication as you explore through your senses. It is also a fun way to connect with other family members as you use your imagination to determine what's in the box.

SUPPLIES

- A cardboard or plastic box
- Small objects found around the home

INSTRUCTIONS

1. Find a box that's big enough to fit different-size objects.

2. Decide who will be the first person to pick the items for the box. The children in the family may want to join forces and choose things for the adults to guess.

3. Look around the house for things to put in the box. You'll want to choose different textures, shapes, and sizes. You might include a book, a small toy, a stuffed animal, a car key, or a napkin. Be sure to inform the kids that the items shouldn't be too sharp, wet, or slimy!

4. Decide who will be the first person to guess what's in the box. That person will close their eyes and give it a go. If the person is comfortable with the idea, you can blindfold them.

5. After they are through guessing, have the person open their eyes (or remove their blindfold) so that they can see what was in the box. Then they get to be the next one to fill the box.

Let's Talk About It: Deciding what to put in the box is always fun, but putting your hand in the box is always a surprise! How easy was it to guess what was in the box? What surprised you about this activity? What did you learn about making assumptions?

For Next Time: Divide the family into teams or put on gloves or oven mitts and see if you can still guess what the objects are.

The Art of Doing Two Things at Once

Charades is a game of nonverbal communication that enhances your ability to understand others through their gestures and expressions. In newer blended families, this game helps people read the signs and signals of their family members, deepening their understanding of one another, and is also a great way to get laughter going. If you decide to team up in this activity, the collaboration helps family members feel closer as you bond through your creative imaginations.

SUPPLIES

- Index cards or paper
- Scissors
- Assorted pens, colored pencils, or markers

INSTRUCTIONS

1. Have the whole family help create the game cards, pairing off younger kids with older ones who can help them. Using index cards or sheets of blank paper cut in small pieces, write the following actions on each card. These are not things you would normally do together—and that's the fun part! Try coming up with your own actions as well.

- Do the limbo
- Read a book
- Put a baby to sleep
- Make a loud sneeze
- Row a boat
- Blow out birthday candles
- Play soccer
- Make a campfire
- Tap dance
- Ride a roller coaster
- Brush teeth
- Iron clothes
- Surf waves
- Dodge the rain

2. Once you have the actions written down, each person draws two cards from the pile and takes a turn performing both scenes simultaneously. For example, someone could draw "ride a roller coaster" and "brush teeth," and they would need to combine the two actions into one scene. The observers must guess what they are doing. The person who guesses correctly gets to go next. If no one guesses within 2 minutes, the actor draws two more cards and performs a new scene.

3. Go over the rules with everyone:

- The person acting out the scenes cannot talk.

- The person acting out the scenes cannot point.

- The person acting out the scenes may only gesture to act out what's on the cards.

- Each person has 2 minutes to act out the scenes on the cards.

- Alternate turns until each person has had an opportunity.

Let's Talk About It: Charades helps spark creative thinking and build collaboration. How easy was it to guess your partner's scene? What would have made it easier to guess? How could you change the rules for a different version of the game? Brainstorming additional scene ideas can be a fun activity in itself. What other scenes would you add to this activity? What did you notice about nonverbal communication in this activity?

For Next Time: Try acting out three different things for a challenge. Invite relatives or friends over for an even bigger, livelier game. If you have a larger gathering, you can work in pairs or two groups. You can also play the game with points and have someone keep track of the score. Whoever guesses the actions correctly first gets two points. If no one guesses correctly, the actor picks up one point.

Where in the World Are You?

Through nonverbal communication, everyone gets to work together in this activity. This is a great team builder that helps improve a blended family's bond. One person pretends to be somewhere, and the rest of the family must guess where they are and then join them. This activity encourages cooperation between family members as you try to interpret the scene and enhance it with a new action. This helps the whole family work together and complement one another's imaginations, reducing feelings of jealousy or animosity.

INSTRUCTIONS

1. Decide who will go first. This person gets to choose the environment they will create. For example, setting up a tent, baking a cake, building a table, or painting a mural.

2. Without saying anything, the person mimes something that would happen in that environment. Maybe they are cooking in the kitchen, playing baseball, or in the middle of a card game.

3. As soon as someone else recognizes where they are, they can join them by doing a complementary action but without saying anything. They may not have guessed correctly, but they can still join in if they think they know what the first person is doing.

4. Eventually, each family member should join in by miming something in the scene.

5. Once everyone has joined the scene and contributed to the action for a couple of minutes, stop the scene. The family members who joined the scene take turns saying where they thought the person who started the original action was.

6. Whether or not everyone ends up in the same environment, this activity will get some laughter going.

Let's Talk About It: In this activity, each family member could end up doing something quite different from the person who started the scene. Did everyone guess correctly, or did someone think they were somewhere other than where the original person intended? How easy or difficult was it to guess where the person was? What clues were helpful in determining where the scene took place? The more you play this game, the more creative you become. What other environments could you choose? If you played this game for several rounds, did it get easier to guess where the scene took place? What would make this game easier or more difficult?

For Next Time: The goal of this activity is to work together by complementing the other person's action, whether they are baking a cake or building a house. If this game is challenging for some family members, pair up to make it easier. Have one pair talk quietly among themselves and decide what the scene will be. Once they start the scene, the other pair or pairs discuss what they think the pair is doing and then join them with a complementary action. For a similar activity, have your family form a circle. One person goes into the center of the circle and mimes a simple activity. The next person comes into the circle and asks the first person, "What are you doing?" The first person answers with something other than what they are actually doing. For example, if they are fishing, they might say, "I'm brushing my teeth." The second person then pretends they are brushing their teeth. The third person comes into the circle and asks the mime, "What are you doing?" It continues in this way until everyone has joined the circle.

Create Your Own Cookie

This activity is a fun way to be both imaginative and creative as you take educated guesses about how a cookie is made. In a large family, you can divide into teams and make two different types of cookies and decide which one you like best. If you have a family with one or two children, the adults can help the kids make a cookie of their choice—without a recipe! Depending on the age of your children, try to let the kids have more of the decision-making power in this process. Mealtimes and cooking can be tense in families, so it's good to have moments where children can experiment with food and have the power to make decisions about how things are concocted.

SUPPLIES

Baking ingredients commonly found in cookies, such as:

- Flour
- Sugar
- Eggs
- Butter
- Baking powder
- Baking soda
- Vanilla extract
- Chocolate chips
- Walnuts (unless someone has a nut allergy)

INSTRUCTIONS

1. Depending on the size of your family, decide if you'll work in teams or as one group.

2. If they are old enough, let the children take charge and decide what they want to put in their cookie, without using a recipe. This will be an experiment for everyone!

3. Use basic cookie ingredients as you create a recipe from memory. Experiment with flour, sugar, eggs, butter, and baking powder. You might want to throw in some chocolate chips or walnuts. Some kids may want to get creative with other ingredients you have on hand, such as raisins, oatmeal, or sprinkles.

4. Preheat the oven. How hot does everyone want to set the oven?

5. Make the batter and place it onto baking sheets. How much? How large should the cookies be?

6. Place the baking sheet into the preheated oven and decide how long you'll bake the cookies.

7. When the cookies have baked for the desired time, remove them from the oven and set aside to cool.

8. Conduct taste tests!

Let's Talk About It: Letting kids explore in the kitchen without too much adult input can be delicious and nerve racking. As an adult, was it hard not to control the process? How did the cookies turn out? Which ingredients would you take out and which ingredients would you add next time? What did you notice about your cookies? Were they thin and crunchy or light and chewy? The ingredients determine the texture and quality of the cookie. If you weren't pleased with the cookie, what could you do differently next time? If you made different cookies next time, what would you make?

For Next Time: Try replacing one or more ingredients. You could also try making other meals this way. How about pancakes or muffins without a mix or recipe? Or let the children in your family who are old enough decide on the dinner menu together, go shopping, and cook a creative meal together. There are also good opportunities to talk about measurement while creating your own cookie. How much of each ingredient did you use and how does changing the measurement or eliminating an ingredient affect the cookie? Cooking together is a good way for siblings and other family members to connect. Occasionally turning the kitchen over to kids who are old enough (with a little adult supervision) lets children take charge in an environment that is sometimes off-limits. Letting them freely experiment in the kitchen can help children develop a love of cooking and help them expand their palates.

CHAPTER FIVE

Chase Adventure

When families embark on a fun adventure, they open the possibility for new social, cognitive, and sensory experiences. Adventures build a child's self-confidence as well as their ability to focus and plan. Excited by the prospect of an adventure, children are more likely to look for new and creative solutions in challenging situations and to persist with difficult tasks. In this chapter, you'll find activities that help your family get active, do everyday things in a different way, and bond with other family members. While some activities are a fun way to explore new settings, other activities help families break from their regular routine and unite around a common purpose.

Dinner Picnic

Dinnertime can be difficult for any family, but unexpressed feelings can dominate mealtime in blended families—whether it's refusing to eat what a stepparent has cooked or noticing that other loved ones are missing from the table. Kids love novelty, and a Dinner Picnic takes everyone out of the normal routine and changes the scene.

SUPPLIES

- Plates
- Utensils
- Napkins
- Food for dinner
- Blanket or outside chairs

INSTRUCTIONS

1. Come together with the family and decide what you'll eat on your picnic and where you'll go. Let each person choose something they'd like to eat or drink, within limits of cost and availability.

2. Decide where you'll eat. Will it be in a nearby park, a lake, the beach, your backyard, or possibly even your bedroom?

3. When the time has come, have the whole family help prepare the food and gather the items that are needed. Give jobs to your children like cutting up vegetables, making sandwiches, or packing the utensils and napkins. Give each child a bag to carry.

4. Don't forget to plan your cleanup, too.

Let's Talk About It: What was your favorite part about the Dinner Picnic? What kind of food would you choose for next time? Would you do this at a different time of day? Where would you go next time?

For Next Time: Have a meal and a movie in the car—making your own drive-in movie theater. Or invite a relative or friend to join you on your Dinner Picnic.

Mystery Photo

In this activity, children and parents create teams to take photos around the home and in the neighborhood. The key is to do it in a way that leaves the viewers guessing. Maybe you snap a picture of a cat's ear, a closeup of a petal, or the wood on a fence. This activity will get your creative juices flowing and everyone wondering what's in the Mystery Photo!

SUPPLIES
* 2 digital cameras or cell phones with cameras

INSTRUCTIONS
1. Divide your family into teams and decide on a prize. Depending on how many people are in your family and what the dynamics are, you could have adults versus children or a stepparent with a stepchild. Decide what makes sense in your family.

2. One person on the team should have a camera (smartphones are fine). Spend time taking pictures inside your home and in the neighborhood. You could even take this activity to a nearby park, beach, or woodsy area for more adventure.

3. Plan a time to come together and share the photos. Each team has to guess what the other team's photos are of. Whoever gets the most correct wins!

Let's Talk About It: The purpose of Mystery Photo is to keep the other team guessing. How well did you work together with your teammate(s)? Did you find it easy or difficult to take pictures in such a way that the subject was unclear? Which one was the hardest to guess and why?

For Next Time: Try doing this activity at night! Or take pictures of things that start with the letter A, or only photograph things that are red. Come up with your own creative categories.

Around Town Scavenger Hunt

Discover new places and interesting facts about where you live. In this scavenger hunt, children enhance their critical thinking skills while all members of your family can collaborate and work toward a common goal as you discover places you have never been. This activity will help blended family members feel grounded in their home and work together as they discover new information about their town or city. Scavenger hunts invite families to discover new things, not only about the place they live, but also about other family members as you plan together, ask questions of one another, and learn new facts about your local digs.

INSTRUCTIONS

1. Use the internet to explore your town or city. As a family, write the answers to the following questions:

- What is the tallest building in your city?

- What is the nearest body of water (a lake, beach, river, or creek)?

- What is the oldest restaurant or eatery in your area?

- What is your city's most popular landmark or building? If you're in a small town, this could be the most popular place that people gather.

- What is an interesting fact from another century about the place you live?

- What is the name of a hiking trail nearby that you've never walked on?

- What is a place nearby that serves a treat with chocolate in it?

- Where is the nearest slide?

- What is a bird that is most often seen in your area?

- Where is the closest fire or police station?

2. Once you've uncovered the information in step 1, decide on two places you'd like to visit or explore. Your family may want to eat at the oldest restaurant, walk to a local landmark, or explore a new hiking trail.

Let's Talk About It: **Even if you've lived somewhere for many years, there is usually something you haven't discovered and probably many historical facts you haven't uncovered about the place you live. What's something new you learned in this activity? Where is a place you would visit again? Can you think of another place in your city or town you've never explored? What else would you add to the scavenger hunt? Did you gain a new appreciation or understanding of your city or town?**

For Next Time: **Try a photo scavenger hunt. Together, brainstorm a list of things to photograph and hit the road. Your list could include: a piece of public art, ice cream from your local creamery, unusual architecture in your area, and the most common bird in your town. Divide your family into teams and see who can come back first with their photos. You can create a scavenger hunt using any theme. You may want to search for a variety of different bugs or animals in your area. You could also do a beach or tide pool scavenger hunt, or search for plants and flowers in your neighborhood. Try visiting as many places as possible in your area that have public art. You can even do a scavenger hunt in your own home!**

Bubbles at the Beach!

Bring your homemade bubbles on a nearby adventure. This recipe makes bigger, thicker bubbles that don't evaporate immediately. While this activity is best suited for a family with younger kids, if there are older children in the mix, they might have fun blowing a few bubbles themselves. Every family needs lighthearted, child-friendly games, especially during an adventure! Children love when adults can tap into their inner kid and blow bubbles, too. In fact, it can help to reduce power struggles and defiance. Don't forget a picnic lunch or snacks.

SUPPLIES

- Dishpan, large bucket, or bowl
- ½ cup sugar
- 4 cups warm water
- ½ cup dish soap
- ½ cup cornstarch (optional)
- 1 tablespoon baking powder (optional)
- Food coloring (optional)
- Needle-nose pliers (optional)
- Wire coat hangers, pipe cleaners, or other objects found around your home that would make good bubble wands (see "For Next Time")

INSTRUCTIONS
CONCOCT YOUR BUBBLE SOLUTION

1. Find a clean dishpan, bucket, or bowl and stir the sugar into the warm water until it dissolves. Add the dish soap and whisk.

2. You can also try adding a little cornstarch, baking powder, or food coloring to enhance your bubble mixture, but these ingredients are not necessary. If any excess foam forms, gently remove it from the bowl.

MAKE THE BUBBLE WAND

3. Using a needle-nose pliers or another tool, untwist and straighten the wire hanger.

4. Use the pliers or your hands to form a circle at one end of the hanger or pipe cleaner. The circle should be about 3 inches or larger in diameter.

5. Twist the wire to close the circle. Leave enough length on one end for the handle.

6. Seal the bubble mixture in a container that will travel well and head off to the beach or a nearby park.

Let's Talk About It: There are lots of ways to make bubble wands. What are some other materials you have around the house that would make good wands? The quality of the bubble depends on your ingredients. What did you notice about your bubbles? What size bubbles did you make? How long did they last? If you experimented with other ingredients, which concoction made the best bubbles?

For Next Time: There are other ingredients you can add to your bubble recipe. Try adding glycerin or corn syrup instead of table sugar to the mix. These sweeteners will produce bigger bubbles that will last even longer. And there are many things that you can blow a bubble with. Do a quick search around your home for objects like a paper clip, a milk carton, a cookie cutter, or a string tied in a loop. Let your kids hunt for other objects that make good wands. You might also try a plastic slotted spoon or a Wiffle ball to blow from. Although regular bubbles have a nice sparkle of their own, adding food coloring to the mix makes bright, beautiful bubbles. Things can get messy quickly. You may want to whisk up your bubble brew outside!

A Volunteer Adventure

Volunteering can be done any time of the year, and it's a great way to help a blended family bond as you work toward a common goal. Volunteering in your community or at your school or helping neighbors on your block will help the whole family learn about one another's skills and interests. Some studies even suggest that volunteering can improve your mood while reducing depression and anxiety—mental health issues that can increase for stepparents. Practical, hands-on activities that the whole family can do together are a great way to realize that you can make a difference in your neighborhood or community and that your efforts matter.

INSTRUCTIONS

1. Come together with your family and brainstorm some options for volunteering. As you're discussing the possibilities, remember that it can be a one-time event, a regular activity, or a seasonal effort.

2. Find out what issues or causes are important to each person in the family. What do the kids feel passionate about? Do a go-around so that each person gets to answer this question. There are many issues to consider. While helping animals may be important to one person, stocking the local food pantry may be of interest to another.

3. After you brainstorm what your passions are, find out what's possible in your area and make a plan. That might involve calling someone at the local animal shelter or going online to find out what the volunteer opportunities are there.

HERE ARE SOME OPTIONS FOR VOLUNTEERING THAT YOU MAY WANT TO CONSIDER:

- Organize a school supply drive.
- Help stock the local food pantry.
- Make valentine cards for the residents of a retirement home.
- Participate in a local cleanup day.
- Pick up litter.
- Help with a community garden project.
- Donate hair to children who are going through chemotherapy.
- Cook a meal for a neighbor who is sick or homebound.

Let's Talk About It: Volunteering for a common cause has many benefits for a blended family. In most cases, it allows you to work as a team, solving problems together and supporting one another. Often when you volunteer, you meet new people, some of whom may be very different from you. This aspect alone helps you expand your experiences and decrease the isolation that can form in families. Did you meet new people on your volunteer adventure? What did you learn about yourself in this process? What did you learn about your own family or others? Did you enjoy the volunteering? Was anything difficult or challenging about it? What would you do differently next time?

For Next Time: If this was a one-time event, you could consider making this a seasonal or regular activity. You might want to branch out and try volunteering for a different organization, or think about how you can help an elderly neighbor or someone who just had a baby. You may have a child who doesn't want to join A Volunteer Adventure. When you notice a child's resistance to joining the family on a special outing, that's the time to spend extra one-on-one time with them. When they feel heard and seen in the family, they are more likely to be flexible and want to come along.

CHAPTER SIX

Think about the Past

In this chapter, you'll find opportunities to reflect on the past and envision the future. Truth Detector (page 58) and A Photo Time Line (page 59) are fun ways to learn about a parent or stepparent's past. Scrapbooks and time capsules let everyone feel seen and know that they hold an important place in the family. When stepparents have trouble finding what they like and appreciate about a stepchild (or vice versa!), sharing A Letter to Self (page 64) will help them build empathy and understanding. Be mindful of your family's past as well. If reflecting on past events will cause children to recall trauma or trigger intense emotions, you will want to be prepared to help them process those reactions and offer support, or you may decide to avoid certain activities entirely.

Truth Detector

This is a fun way to find out about each person's past. Otherwise known as "Two Truths and a Lie," this activity focuses on family history. This exercise will help stepchildren and stepparents get to know one another, and biological family members will find out new and surprising things about everyone.

INSTRUCTIONS

1. One person in the family thinks of two things that are true about their past and one thing that is a lie. The truths may be events or experiences that the rest of the family doesn't know about. Either way, the idea is to come up with two true statements or short stories and one lie.

2. The person then does their best to tell the group their two truths and a lie, in a convincing manner, doing their best to disguise the lie as being a truth.

3. The other members of the family are the truth detectors. They must guess which statements are true and which one is a lie.

4. Give each family member their own opportunity to make their guess, without being talked over or interrupted.

5. The person who guesses accurately gets to be the storyteller next.

Let's Talk About It: You may be surprised about what you learn in your family! You may also find out that stepfamily members share common experiences. How easy was it to guess the truths and the lie? What surprised you the most?

For Next Time: To switch things up a bit, have one parent tell two truths and a lie about their child. A stepparent or stepchild must guess which one is the lie.

A Photo Time Line

Images are a powerful way to connect with the past and with one another. In this activity, kids will put childhood photos of their parents in chronological order, learning about both biological parents and stepparents in the process. This is a good way for members of a blended family to learn about one another's pasts and appreciate their family histories.

SUPPLIES
* Old family photos

INSTRUCTIONS

1. Collect as many family photos as you can from the adults in the family—biological parents and stepparents. This can include pictures of the parent at any age and photos of grandparents and relatives.

2. Come together as a family, lay the photos out on a large table, and mix them up.

3. Have children sort through the photos and put them in chronological order.

4. Hanging family photos around the home helps everyone in the family know that they belong there. This is especially important in blended families when stepchildren or stepparents feel like outsiders.

Let's Talk About It: Questions for the kids can include: How easy was it to guess what order the photos went in? What did you learn? What was something from the past you wish you could experience today? Adults may want to share something from their lives at the time the photo was taken.

For Next Time: If you have pictures of distant relatives, add them to the mix and see how easy it is for the kids to guess who they are. You can also have a stepparent try putting photos of stepchildren into chronological order.

Collecting Memories

Scrapbooks are a great way to record experiences, hobbies, talents, and milestones. In a blended family, it's one way to help everyone feel like they hold an important place in the family as you honor each person's qualities, interests, and achievements. In this version, you'll create a section in a book for each family member to keep their favorite photos and meaningful objects or keepsakes.

SUPPLIES

- An old photo album
- Construction paper
- Card stock
- Assorted pens, colored pencils, and markers
- Photos
- Memorabilia from school
- Glue
- Tape

INSTRUCTIONS

1. Decide what you'll keep your memories in. You might use an old photo album or create a simple book with construction paper or card stock.

2. Depending on how big the scrapbook is and how many people are in the family, decide how many pages will be dedicated to each person. Two pages is a good place to start.

3. Have each person make a list of what they want in their scrapbook. Adults can make a list for younger children. Consider including photos from a favorite family vacation or an adventure at the beach. You could include small keepsakes that represent someone's hobby or interest, such as a guitar pick, a short journal entry, or their latest piece of art. You can also include quotes or favorite sayings.

4. Spread out your items on a large surface. Before you adhere them to the book with tape or glue, have each person decide how they want their items arranged.

5. If you're creating a book from construction paper or card stock, hand out pieces of paper to each person so they can design their section. If you're using a photo album or other large book, you can have one designated designer do the layout once each person has decided on where they'd like things placed. Or each person can have a turn with the scrapbook to work on their section.

Let's Talk About It: **If you're a newly blended family, a scrapbook will help you learn about the other members of your family. What were your favorite things to include in the scrapbook? What did you learn was important to someone else in your family? What part of the activity did you like best? What other scrapbooks could you make?**

For Next Time: **If your family enjoyed this activity, think about creating scrapbooks for specific interests. Maybe your children would like a place to save keepsakes from their favorite school year, their favorite family recipes, or the last vacation. Scrapbooks can also help you process difficult experiences, like the passing of a pet or a loved one. When you put photos and keepsakes together about a grandparent or the family dog who has died, you tell a story about their life that can help you process their passing. Also, consider how your scrapbook can age with you. Each year, you can add an keepsake from a special holiday or event. For example, maybe you want to capture the growth of your children each year by taking a photo of them in the same place every October. Annual scrapbooks are a great way to chart the growth of your family year after year.**

Family Food History

Some people's fondest memories are connected to the smell of a delicious dessert, freshly baked bread, or a meat drenched in a tangy marinade wafting through their childhood home. Family history, culture, and traditions are passed down to family members through food. Food connects you to the people you love. In this activity, you will join forces with another family member to prepare a dish or dessert that was made by your relatives or has cultural significance to you. Whether it's a grandmother's soup, a great-uncle's side dish, or a food that is commonly found in your country of origin, Family Food History invites you to explore what you eat. And if your family is a mix of many cultures, make sure to include everyone by either making multiple dishes in the same meal or setting aside a night for them, too.

SUPPLIES

- Cooking pots and utensils
- Ingredients for the dish or dessert you're making
- Music and tablecloth (optional)

INSTRUCTIONS

1. Depending on the size of your family, divide into pairs so that you have a partner to work with.

2. Each pair should choose a night that they'll cook for the rest of the family. They may decide to cook a full meal, a side dish, or a dessert.

3. If each dish complements the other and can be eaten in the same meal, you might want to share your creations all on the same night.

4. Decide on a recipe that is culturally significant to at least one person in the pair. If a stepparent is pairing up with a stepchild, they'll need to decide if they want to make something from the stepparent's family of origin or from the child's cultural heritage.

5. This activity includes a little research. This could entail calling a relative, such as a grandparent, for a family recipe or finding an authentic recipe online or in the library.

6. The pair should make a list of the ingredients they need and go shopping together.

7. When preparing the dish or dessert, decide which role each person will have. If there are young children in the family, they can chop, stir, drop ingredients into bowls, and grease pans.

8. Once the dish is ready, children can set the table. You may want to create a culturally significant setting with a certain song or special tablecloth.

Let's Talk About It: Cooking together is not only a great opportunity for young children to learn about measurement and develop a joy of cooking but also a great way to connect with other family members. What did you learn about your family or your stepparent's family in this process? What other dishes or desserts could you cook next time? Is there a recipe in your family that already has a special meaning attached to it? What foods or recipes do you associate with good memories?

For Next Time: Not only does cooking together as a family have many benefits, but studies suggest that eating together has multiple positive outcomes as well. When families sit down at the table together, children feel closer and more connected to their parents, and high-risk behaviors and mental health problems decrease. Cooking meaningful dishes together can be a fun and tasty incentive to eat together and a good reminder to do it on a regular basis.

A Letter to Self

Often in blended families, children and stepparents feel lost in the fray and are not sure where they stand. To help family members feel grounded in their families and reflect on their own lives, everyone will write a letter to themselves that they will open in one year. This activity will help you and your family slow down, self-reflect, appreciate the present, and gain insights about the past. A Letter to Self helps you look for the bright spots in your life and appreciate the other members of your family.

SUPPLIES
- Paper
- Pen

INSTRUCTIONS

1. Set a timer for 10 to 15 minutes and have each person take time to respond to the following questions.

- What lessons have you learned or what goals have you completed over the last year? Celebrate your accomplishments!

- What do you want to remember about the present?

- What are your goals for the future?

- What habits do you want to change?

- What do you want to learn?

- What do you want to do more of in the future?

- What are you passionate about?

- What's lighting you up and making you happy right now?

- Where do you want to grow?

- Who is your favorite teacher or mentor right now? What do you like about them?

- What are you looking forward to this year?

2. Once you've done some writing or taken notes using some of the previous questions, set a timer for 15 minutes and write a letter to yourself.

3. When each person has had enough time to write their letter to self, either gather them all together and store them in a special place where you'll remember where they are, or have each person safely store their own letters. For younger children, have parents hold on to them for safekeeping.

4. Come together as a family and open the letters a year later. Have a special meal as you reflect on what you wrote the previous year.

Let's Talk About It: **Letters to yourself help you look forward to the future and appreciate how far you've come. What have you learned over the last year? Did you accomplish your goals? Do you have any new insights about yourself? What did you learn about other people in your family? What inspired you about what other family members wrote in their letter?**

For Next Time: **You could write a letter to another member of the family that they can open next year. Let them know what you appreciate about them, what you're grateful for, and what you'd like to do more of with them in the future. If you have younger children who are not yet writing, they can dictate a letter to an adult. This is a good opportunity to appreciate someone in your family as you let them know what you love about them. Make this a yearly ritual as you come together and share memories about yourself and others.**

CHAPTER SEVEN

Look to the Future

When you focus on a future event, whether it's an upcoming vacation or a civic action in your community, you set your sights on something positive and make your life more meaningful in the present. Research suggests that engaging in future-focused activities can help you be kinder and more generous and leads to more fulfilled lives. When conflict in your blended family shapes your daily interactions and you worry about the future of your relationships, the activities in this chapter will help you curb your concerns and find meaning in the present as you develop leadership skills and get to know your family and community in a new way.

Looking Forward to the Future

Planning fun activities propels you forward with positive energy and helps you create the discipline to do things you're not excited about as you wait for what's to come. In this activity, create a list of the things your family is looking forward to—helping everyone feel seen and heard and happier.

SUPPLIES
- Paper
- Pen

INSTRUCTIONS

1. Assemble a family meeting and explain the purpose of this activity is to plan fun events for the future.

2. Each person makes their own list. Adults can make a list for younger children.

3. Create three categories for cost: free, low cost, and high cost. Try to come up with a few activities for each.

4. Discuss timing for the identified activities. What are things you could do one day after school? What are things you could do on the weekend? What are things that will take more time—such as a longer trip or overnight somewhere?

Let's Talk About It: Focusing on the future is a powerful way to feel more positive about the present. What are you most excited about that you put on the list? Which can you accomplish in the coming weeks? What will take more time and money to plan?

For Next Time: Once everyone has brainstormed a list of activities they'd like to do, take it a step further and do some planning with the whole family. Some activities might not include everyone, and that's okay. For example, both parents can make a date with each child to do something that the child is looking forward to on their list.

The Time Capsule

The Time Capsule preserves the present and helps us envision the future. For blended families, this activity addresses everyone's need for a sense of belonging.

SUPPLIES
- Shoebox or plastic container
- Pen and paper

INSTRUCTIONS

1. Have a family meeting and explain why you want to create a time capsule. It's a great way to set goals, cherish memories, and reflect on the future.

2. Next, pick your container. Will you have one large container for the whole family, or will each person have their own capsule? A shoebox or plastic container is fine as long as it's durable. Remember, you won't open this for some time, 5 or even 10 years.

3. Make a list of the things you want in your capsule like a letter to your future self, a favorite toy or collectible or a newspaper.

4. Add the items (get something from everyone!) to the container.

5. Store it somewhere it won't get moved a lot like a garage or dresser drawer.

Let's Talk About It: **Was there anything that was hard to part with for several years or more? What was most important for you to include in your time capsule?**

A Dream with a Deadline

In this activity, you'll be creating an interest map. An interest map is simply a mind map of the things that someone likes—a graphic representation of their passions and skills. This activity turns each person's interests into goals and aspirations. It will help members of a blended family plan together so they feel like they are moving forward with one another. It helps family members learn more about one another and support their progress as they hold them accountable.

SUPPLIES

- Assorted pens, colored pencils, and markers
- Paper

INSTRUCTIONS

1. Have a family meeting where you all discuss what you enjoy, what you're good at, and what your goals are.

2. Then everyone writes their name in the middle of a piece of paper and circles it. Next, draw a few lines extending out from the circle and write some interests. Then circle those.

3. Once you've written down your interests, draw lines off those and write out ways to develop each interest, then circle them. If you have a love for swimming, for example, you could join a swim team, take lessons, spend more time at a local pool or beach, etc.

4. Continue to fill out as many interest circles and subcircles as you can that show how to increase your skills and keep your interest.

5. Choose three things to be goals for the year. Turn your paper over and write down these three specific things. Then everyone shares their results.

Let's Talk About It: **Setting goals as a family, even if they come from individual interests, can help the whole family move forward together. Goals can transcend the daily stress of family life and help parents and stepparents feel less overwhelmed and run-down as they share excitement about the future. What did you learn about other members of your family? What did you notice about interests, passions, or areas in which they want to expand or develop their skills? If you had to come up with one family goal for the next six months, what would it be? It's important to celebrate your accomplishments, big and small. How will you celebrate when you've achieved one of your goals?**

For Next Time: **Young children can set goals as well. They can take this opportunity to envision the things they want to learn or the passions they want to explore by painting or drawing. You can display their goals, represented in an artistic way, on a wall in your home. And don't forget to track your goals and celebrate along the way! Checking in with your goals is a good topic for a family meeting or a conversation with family members after dinner. Set up small celebrations when each person has reached their goal, or is halfway there, to acknowledge each person's progress.**

Mapping for Social Change

Igniting a family activism project will help everyone feel like they have an important role in the family. Not only will the whole family feel like they have agency as a team, but each person will also know they have the power to make a difference. In this activity, your family will start by "mapping" your community to discover what the issues and pressing needs are. Then you will choose a project that will help address one problem in your neighborhood or city.

SUPPLIES

- Internet (optional)
- Long roll of white paper
- Assorted pens, colored pencils, and markers

INSTRUCTIONS

1. Begin by making a map of your neighborhood or community. Use the internet to help or take a drive together and create the map from memory upon returning home.

2. You'll want to choose some of the following things to add to your map:

- Local schools
- Major streets
- Public transportation routes
- Grocery stores or farmers' markets
- Hospitals or health-care centers
- Shelters (for humans and animals)
- Play spaces for kids
- Animals in your area (wild or domesticated)
- Zoos or aquariums
- Bodies of water: beaches, lakes, or rivers

3. Spread out a long roll of white paper on the floor so the whole family can work on creating the map.

4. Decide which places, people, and animals you want to include from the previous list and what else you might add. Highlight the places you love to go and note places you choose to avoid.

5. Let everyone decide what they want to draw first and then get to work!

6. Once you've drawn a map of your neighborhood or larger community, brainstorm a community action project by exploring these questions:

- What have you heard about or observed that are current issues in your community?

- Are there any people, places, or animals that need help?

- What do you want to change about your neighborhood or community?

- What places could be improved?

Let's Talk About It: Community mapping helps you understand the characteristics of your community, appreciate the assets of your area, and learn more about the challenges facing people, places, and animals where you live. Each member of a newly formed family will have different information and experiences they can contribute to this project. This activity also helps family members find common ground by discussing issues they care about. What is something new you learned about your community? What are some things you enjoy about your city or town? Were there any issues that you uncovered? Are there any major conflicts in your community?

For Next Time: You can pull out the map and add more details to it or use it to inspire a site visit to a place on your map that's of interest to your family. Consider attaching souvenirs or adding illustrations to help capture your adventures and turning your map into a collection of family memories made in your community.

Change the Future through Civic Action

This is a great next step if you made a map of your community in the activity on page 72. And if not, you can jump in right here! Whether you're angry about an injustice, concerned about a situation in your community, or excited to support a cause you care about, this activity will propel your whole family forward as you discover that you have the power to make a difference in your community. Bringing everyone together to work on a cause they care about helps children who are traveling between two homes notice their importance in the family and feel anchored not only in an important project but in the family as well.

INSTRUCTIONS

1. Decide what issue or problem your family wants to tackle. If you didn't do the community mapping in the previous activity, take some time to brainstorm on a sheet of paper an issue that's important to your family and what you could do to bring attention to it and create a change.

2. Discuss the project goals together. What do you hope to accomplish? Maybe you want to gather food and clothing for homeless children or raise money for a city hit by a hurricane. Or maybe you simply want to make cards for people who have had a difficult time lately or cook a large meal and share it with someone in need in your neighborhood. Or you could plan to spend time at your local senior center, hold a car wash to raise money for the cause you're concerned about, or collect blankets and towels for the local animal shelter.

3. Here are some questions to answer as you decide how and where you want to create change:

- What are the long- and short-term goals?

- What challenges might you encounter along the way?

- How will you overcome any challenges you might face?

- What resources and supplies will you need to accomplish your goals?

- When will your project start and when will it end?

Let's Talk About It: **The experience of participating in a civic action project can help families—even its youngest members—know that they can influence the course of events, make a difference in people's lives, and develop a new perspective on what's possible. Do you know the story of Mia Hansen? Only 10 years old, she wasn't happy that her local Jamba Juice was selling her favorite fruit drinks in Styrofoam cups. So, she started a campaign online and ended up with more than 130,000 signatures! Because of her work, Jamba Juice switched from Styrofoam to an eco-friendlier material.**

When thinking about your project, did you encounter any challenges along the way? What would you do differently next time? If you were to do another civic action project, what would it be? This activity connects you to the community around you. Who else might you collaborate with in the future?

For Next Time: **You may want to research another issue and execute another civic action project. Think about specific people, places, and organizations like friends, schools, sports teams, churches, or synagogues that you could collaborate with on a future project. Instead of thinking locally, think globally. How can you set your sights on a bigger project with even more impact?**

CHAPTER EIGHT

Boost Your Brainpower

Get ready for a brain workout! The activities in this chapter are sure to boost your mental acuity and activate your neural circuits! In addition to boosting your memory, increasing your problem-solving skills, and tapping into your creativity to win the challenge, these games each have a competitive edge. In blended families, competition can run high. But having a safe and fun space within the family to challenge one another, make mistakes, and cheer others on can increase the bonds between all members of the family. The skills required in the games in this chapter—observation, critical thinking, listening, and working together—can help nurture relationships in a blended family and increase cooperation and connection with lighthearted competition.

What Changed?

This is a fun activity that can be played anywhere at home. Blended families can enjoy a friendly competition that requires focus and observation. Plus, taking turns and listening to one another helps build better listeners and observers in everyday family interactions.

INSTRUCTIONS

1. Gather everyone in the room and decide who will go first. Then have everyone else take a good look around the room, memorize what they see, and close their eyes (or leave the room).

2. The rearranger has three minutes to change four objects in the room. Items can be moved but not hidden.

3. When they are done, ask everyone to open their eyes (or return to the room). Each player takes turns guessing. The changer will simply answer "Yes" or "No" in response to whether the person has guessed all four items correctly, but should not give hints.

4. The person who guesses all four things correctly will get to be the changer next. If no one guesses all four items correctly, the changer gets to take another turn.

5. You can set a number of points, or rounds, or a time limit to determine when the game ends.

Let's Talk About It: **What did you like about the game? What rules would you change to make the game more fun? How could you work in teams next time? What strategies did you use to guess which items changed?**

For Next Time: **Try this for another version: One at a time, have each person go in and change one thing. Then everyone goes back into the room and tries to guess what the others have changed.**

DIY Matching Memory Game!

Memory games are a great way to increase your attention, concentration, focus, and long-term memory. Memory games also call on everyone's patience and require taking turns and showing respect—the cornerstone of healthy families.

SUPPLIES

- Scissors
- Cardboard or poster board
- Paper
- Glue
- Ruler
- Assorted pens, colored pencils, and markers

INSTRUCTIONS

1. Cut the cardboard to the same size as the paper and glue together.

2. After the glue has dried, use the ruler to make a grid of equal-size boxes on the cardboard. It should look like a tic-tac-toe box.

3. Have the children draw matching pairs of pictures within all the boxes (such as two cats, two hearts, etc.) then cut them out.

4. Arrange the cards on a flat surface, with the creative side (drawings/words) facing down.

5. The youngest person goes first and turns over two cards. If they match, the player picks them up and takes another turn. If not, the player turns them facedown again and the next player goes.

6. The game ends when all the cards are gone. The winner is the person with the most pairs.

For Next Time: **The more cards, the more difficult it is, so keep it small if playing with younger kids. Conversely, consider drawing pairs of things that are similar, but not identical, for an extra challenge. For example, you can have two types of fruit that make a pair—an apple and an orange.**

Quick Wins

Silly, creative, and fabulously fun, these one-minute activities are perfect for an indoor game day. Like the *Minute to Win It* game show, you have 60 seconds to achieve tasks like balancing dice, stacking cans, or picking up pasta without using your hands. These one-minute challenges are harder than you'd think but offer plenty of opportunities for everyone to be a winner. A recurring game night can be a fun ritual, something that's extra important to blended families, as they anchor the family together around a fun routine.

SUPPLIES

- 20 plastic cups
- Petroleum jelly
- Cotton balls
- 2 bowls
- 1 ice-pop stick or ruler
- 5 pairs of dice
- 3 Ping-Pong balls
- 1 cup
- 4 paper plates
- 1 strand of uncooked spaghetti
- 6 pieces of penne pasta

INSTRUCTIONS

Here are five 60-second challenges for the whole family. First, set up the materials for each activity. Then set your timer and move through the challenges one by one.

1. **Stack Attack:** Using 20 paper or plastic cups, each family member gets 60 seconds to stack the cups in a pyramid and then unstack them back into a single stack. The best time wins!

2. **A Sticky Nosedive:** With petroleum jelly dabbed on your nose, move cotton balls from one bowl to another. The challenge is to pick up five cotton balls with your nose and move them to a different bowl in 60 seconds—no hands allowed!

3. **Tumbling Dice:** In this activity, you'll divide into pairs for a quick balancing challenge. While one person holds an ice-pop stick or ruler in their mouth, the other person will stack as many dice as possible on the stick in 60 seconds. (If you don't have dice around, use any small objects that balance on an ice-pop stick instead.)

4. **Bouncy Balls:** Each player will stand on a chair and drop three Ping-Pong balls into a cup on the floor. The goal is to get all three balls in the cup without missing a shot and without any bouncing out.

5. **A Tricky Noodle:** In this challenge, you'll put one strand of uncooked spaghetti in your mouth and try to pick up six pieces of uncooked penne pasta and place them in a bowl. The trick is not to use your hands!

Let's Talk About It: A challenge with a timer involved usually gets the energy flowing and lots of people laughing. Quick games like these are a great opportunity for family members to collaborate creatively and cheer one another on. But the competition can be stressful. Make sure you rotate teams occasionally to alleviate the intensity of the challenge as these types of games can elicit high spirits!

Which one was your favorite 60-second challenge? Which one did you find most challenging? What are some other creative challenges you can think of? What would be a fun way to combine two or more of the challenges?

For Next Time: These challenges can be adapted for children of different ages. For younger children, make the challenge simpler and provide more time. For example, you can reduce the number of cups to make Stack Attack easier. For older children and adults, you can increase the number of items in each challenge. You could also have teams work together to develop cooperation among family members.

The Spaghetti Marshmallow Challenge

The goal of this activity is to build the tallest, sturdiest structure that will hold a marshmallow. Using spaghetti, tape, and a marshmallow for the top, you have 20 minutes to create your masterpiece. Dividing your family into teams for a fun competition is a good way to build relationships among family members who might not interact much. This activity calls on everyone's creative and cognitive skills!

SUPPLIES

Each pair gets:
- 25 sticks of dry spaghetti
- 3-foot strip of masking tape
- 1 marshmallow

For everyone to share:
- Timer
- Measuring tape

INSTRUCTIONS

1. Divide your family into two- to three-person teams (more teams = more fun). This is a good opportunity to split into pairs of family members who haven't yet formed close bonds, because building the tower calls for lots of teamwork and collaboration. You'll also want to have someone keep track of the time and let everyone know when there are 10 minutes left and 2 minutes left.

2. Each pair gets 25 sticks of spaghetti, 3 feet of masking tape, and a marshmallow.

3. Each pair may want to build on a separate table or in another room to avoid any shaking or conflicts among teams.

4. Your team will have 20 minutes to construct a tower of spaghetti and tape that can hold a marshmallow.

5. You're not allowed to use any other supplies than the ones given.

6. You can break the spaghetti into smaller pieces if you'd like, but once your original pieces have been broken, you can't have more spaghetti.

7. Your entire marshmallow must be placed on top of the tower (no spearing it with spaghetti). A marshmallow that has been cut or munched doesn't count!

8. When the timer goes off, measure your creation from the surface of the table to the top of the marshmallow tower. The team with the tallest tower standing with a marshmallow on top wins. Don't forget to enjoy your snack at the end!

Let's Talk About It: Everyone wants to avoid that moment when their tower comes crashing down under the weight of a marshmallow. In this activity, you have to use your best problem-solving and collaboration skills, as it challenges you to iterate the process and learn from mistakes. What strategy did you use? What worked well? What was challenging about this activity? Did you work well together as a team? What would you do differently next time? What other materials could you use to construct the tower?

For Next Time: Omit the tape and use only marshmallows and spaghetti to build a tower. Or try using small index cards to build a tower. Can you build something with index cards alone? If not, add some paper clips into the mix and notice the difference. Then try making the tallest tower you can out of index cards. Next, try making a strong tower of index cards—one that could hold a book! Look around your home and find other materials to build a tower with. Experiment with setting the timer for different amounts of time and see what happens!

Spiral Math

A fun competition can have a lasting impact that everyone remembers for years to come. Spiral Math is an exciting way for young people in the family to practice their math skills. It's an opportunity for adults to not only get a sense of their children's mathematical abilities but also to sharpen their own skills in preparation for homework help. If you need a fresh idea for a family card game, Spiral Math is it. This activity will be a welcome addition to your family's favorite card games.

SUPPLIES

- 1 deck of cards with the face cards removed
- 1 die
- Game pieces

INSTRUCTIONS

1. Spread the cards out, facedown, in a winding or spiral path. This will be your playing board. You can use the same spiral each time you play or change the design of the cards for each game. The object of the game is to be the first person to move from start to finish.

2. Decide who will go first by a roll of the die. The person with the highest number starts.

3. The roll of a die determines how many spaces the player can move. If the player rolls a four, they move four cards ahead. When they reach the fourth card, they must multiply the number they rolled by the number on the playing card. If they get the answer right, they stay there.

4. Each person takes turns rolling the die and moving their piece around the spiral. If you land on a card with another player on it, you bump that person to the beginning of the board.

5. If the number on your die and the number on your playing card where you land are the same, it's called a double and you get to go again. For example, if you roll a five on your die and land on a five (and multiply those numbers correctly) you get to take another turn.

6. The first person who lands on the last card and answers it correctly wins. You need to roll the exact number to get there. If you don't, then roll again on your next turn.

Let's Talk About It: This activity is a good opportunity for school-aged members of the family to practice their math skills, and adults can build communication skills that will be useful for homework help later. For adults and older siblings—what tricks did you learn to memorize your multiplication tables that you might pass on to the younger members of your family? Which problems do you need to spend more time memorizing?

For Next Time: For younger children who are not yet multiplying, you can change the operation to addition or subtraction. Another option is to place all cards facedown and practice number recognition by simply moving forward along the game board with the number that you roll on the die and moving your piece along the board. You can also change the rules so that the player must specify which operation to use when combining the number of the card and the die. And if you want your children to practice their math skills, offer a big prize for the winner.

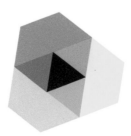

CHAPTER NINE

Stay Active

Being active is one of the best ways to bring everyone together. The following activities let each person engage according to their age and ability, which is especially important in a blended family when some people may feel left out because they don't have the skills to perform a particular sport or activity that unites other family members. This is doubly true for members with disabilities, so you may need to modify according to your family's needs. After all, these activities are meant to let members of a blended family support one another. They'll cheer one another on as they jump through an obstacle course, throw Frisbees on the ground to make a win, and join forces to juggle balls in the air. Active games also allow family members to show care and connection in a nonverbal way, which can be especially helpful for younger children.

A Chalk Obstacle Course

This is a good way for younger kids to use their gross motor skills, for the whole family to get a little exercise, and for blended families to get outside and enjoy some movement and challenge together.

SUPPLIES
- Sidewalk chalk or masking tape

INSTRUCTIONS

1. In this activity, you make a single line using chalk or masking tape for the base of the course. This is the line everyone will follow.

2. When designing your course, here are some things to consider:

- Small circles can be used as stepping-stones, while larger circles are spread out for jumping.

- Rectangles indicate hurdles to jump over.

- Draw swirls to make players spin in a circle.

- Add other shapes and rules, too!

- Create a starting and ending point and follow the line to the finish as you stick to the rules of the shapes.

Let's Talk About It: Young children will love this game, and adults will get a little extra exercise as they move through the obstacle course. What other shapes and rules can you add to the activity? Did you use a special strategy to get to the end? What was the hardest part of the course? If anyone in the family uses a wheelchair, create a path that they can maneuver through using the chalk or masking tape.

For Next Time: Try holding hands with another family member as you go through the obstacle course. If you have older children in your family, you can enlist them in designing the course. For very young children, try placing a stuffed animal or object at the end for a fun reward.

The Big Blowdown

Kids will love this fun balloon challenge. Focus and hand-eye coordination are a must. This activity allows teammates to bond as they try different strategies for success.

SUPPLIES

- Tape or string
- Table
- 15 paper cups
- 1 balloon per person

INSTRUCTIONS

1. Divide the family into two teams. Each team is given the same number of balloons, even if the team sizes are different.

2. Use tape or string to divide a table in half, then build a tower of cups on the line.

3. Have each team member inflate a balloon and hold it shut. Don't tie it.

4. Each person then holds their balloon and aims the end at the tower of cups.

5. On the count of three, release the air in the balloons and use it to blow cups over to the opponent's side. Count how many cups have fallen on each side of the line. The team with the lowest score wins.

6. Suggested rules:

   - No blowing the cups.
   - No touching the table.
   - Cups that fall on the ground will not be counted.

Let's Talk About It: This is a high-energy game, so make sure you have enough room for flying cups! How could you build the structure to make the game more fun? How did you work together? Did each person have a different role or position in the game?

For Next Time: Try dividing the table into four squares and set up the cups in a cross pattern. For an easier game, use fewer cups.

Group Juggle

In this noncompetitive activity, blended families can come together to build trust and cooperation as they work to make sure they are throwing the balls in the right order. This activity invites members of a blended family to put aside their personal agendas and work as a team.

SUPPLIES

* 4 to 6 balls, beanbags, or rolled-up pairs of socks

INSTRUCTIONS

1. Have your family form a circle. Throw one ball, beanbag, or sock to someone in the circle and say their name as you throw it.

2. The person who received the ball will then throw it to someone else as they say the name of the person they are throwing it to. It will continue until each person has caught and thrown the ball once.

3. Ask each person to identify who they received the ball from and who they threw it to. Once you've done one round of this, stop and let your family know they will need to remember who threw the ball to them and who they are throwing it to.

4. Do a second round like this by throwing the ball in the same pattern to the same people as you say their name out loud. But this time the leader will throw another ball into the game after the first ball has been thrown to the third person in the circle. At this point, you'll have two balls going in the same order.

5. The leader will continue to add balls and throw them in the same order until lots of balls are flying through the circle. The challenge is keeping your eye on the balls as they fly!

Let's Talk About It: **To keep the balls in the air and moving in the right direction, families must work collaboratively. Using positive communication, family members support one another to catch flying balls and pick up ones that have gone astray. What did you like about this activity? What did you find challenging? How many balls in the circle were too many balls? What could you use besides small, soft balls for another round?**

For Next Time: **This activity can be played at any age. The key is to change the objects being thrown according to the skill levels in your family. With a large family, you can also play Zigzag Juggle. Have family members line up facing one another. The person at the end of the line begins the game by throwing in a ball. The ball is then thrown in a zigzag pattern down the line. Each family member must catch and throw each ball at least twice. If you want to make things even more challenging, try throwing a ball in the reverse order while you have the balls flying in the original order. If you have younger children in your family, you may want to use fewer balls. With older children, try making the game more diffi-cult by throwing in larger balls or increase the number of balls.**

DIY Bowling Game

This DIY Bowling Game will get everyone moving! Play it inside on a rainy day or move it outside when the weather permits. Though it's geared toward younger children, everyone from toddlers to teens—and even babies and adults—loves the satisfaction of knocking over a row of plastic bottles. This is a great way for families to work together, encourage one another, and get some giggles going.

SUPPLIES

- 6 plastic water bottles
- Paint
- Water
- An indoor ball for bowling (a tennis ball, foam ball, or other bouncy ball)

INSTRUCTIONS

1. In this activity, everyone will use their creativity to design their own bowling pins. In this version, you'll use plastic bottles, but other alternatives are offered later in "For Next Time."

2. Your local bowling alley will use 10 pins, but for an indoor game on a rainy day, 6 works well, too.

3. Gather recycled water bottles and give them an extra rinse to make sure they are clean inside.

4. Drop a small amount of paint in each bottle (about 2 tablespoons). Each bottle should be a different color. Add a little water (about 2 teaspoons) if it isn't runny enough.

5. Put the caps back on and shake each bottle to coat the inside.

6. When you're done shaking, pour out any excess water. Remove the cap and let the paint dry overnight or for as long as necessary. If you're worried about anyone opening the bottles in the future, you can always glue the cap back on.

7. Once they are dry, set up the bowling pins in a 1-2-3 triangle formation. If you're playing inside, find a good indoor ball to use.

8. Place a piece of tape where the bowlers will stand.

9. Decide how many rounds you'll play (10 is traditional), then who will go first. If you knock down all the pins on the first roll, you bowled a strike and your turn is over. If you do it in two rolls, you bowled a spare.

10. Each pin that is knocked down is worth one point. Strikes get an extra three points, spares an extra one. The winner is the person who has the most points.

Let's Talk About It: With this activity, there are no limits on who can bowl—it's low-impact and easy to learn. Not only will this activity help you work on your flexibility and balance, but you'll also get to practice good hand-eye coordination at the same time. How did it go when you created your own bowling pins? Did you run into any challenges? Where was the best place in your home to set up the activity? Where else could you play? How easy was it to get a strike?

For Next Time: For much younger kids, you can scrap the previous game instructions and have fun simply knocking down pins with a ball. You can also get creative and find other things around your home to use as bowling pins. Try other plastic or lightweight containers for bowling pins or make your own out of used paper towel tubes that are cut in half and decorated.

Frisbee Tic-Tac-Toe

If you like logic and strategy mixed with a little anticipation, you'll like Frisbee Tic-Tac-Toe. It's also a great way to practice your throw. Landing a disc on a specific square in front of you will likely be a challenge for young people and adults alike. This is a great way to level the playing field for all members of the family and have some fun at the same time. This game is also great to carry along on a family excursion or trip.

SUPPLIES

- A blanket, tablecloth, or large piece of cloth about the size of a shower curtain
- Painter's tape (optional)
- Chalk (optional)
- 6 Frisbees (3 of one color, 3 of another color)

INSTRUCTIONS

1. Have your family help set up the tic-tac-toe board. Spread out a large blanket or piece of cloth on the ground. If you don't have material to spare, you can skip this part and just use tape or chalk in the next step.

2. Use painter's tape to create a large 3x3 tic-tac-toe board on the blanket or ground. If don't have a blanket for the board, simply draw the tic-tac-toe board on a large cement driveway or on a quiet street with chalk.

3. Draw a line using chalk or painter's tape to throw from and decide who will go first. Each person takes turns throwing a disc with the intent of landing three in a row on the board (up and down, across, or diagonally).

4. Once a square is occupied, no other player can land there. Anything that lands on an occupied square must be thrown again.

5. Whoever gets three in a row wins!

Let's Talk About It: It can take time to learn how to throw a disc, and getting it to a specific spot on the ground is no piece of cake, either. This is a great way to get out of the house and practice your throwing skills. What helped you in this activity? What was most challenging about it? What would you do differently next time? What other types of game boards could you create on the ground or in your home? What other types of objects could you use besides Frisbees that would work well in this game?

For Next Time: If you don't have six Frisbees available, try using disposable container tops, cardboard cutouts, or plastic plates. Get creative as you make your own Frisbees by using markers, paints, and stickers. Tic-tac-toe is a great game to play anywhere. Try making a portable tic-tac-toe game that you can bring to a picnic or entertain the kids with on an airplane. Find small rocks in your neighborhood or a nearby park that would make good game pieces. Paint them different colors, draw an "X" on three rocks and an "O" on three other rocks. Try using a piece of wood or even a picnic table for the game board.

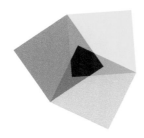

CHAPTER TEN

Tell the Truth

Both serious and silly, these activities will have you sharing deep reflections about moral issues or deciding whether to visit a space station or the bottom of the ocean. They all invite family members to consider important issues, share personal experiences, or imagine something different. When all family members are asked how they feel or where they stand on important topics, it begins to close the insider/outsider gap as everyone feels important and heard. While some activities will develop trust and understanding, others may incite laugher.

What Did You Do This Week?

In this activity, everyone will draw pictures of things they did that week while the others have to guess what happened. This is a fun and easy way to build closeness among family members. It doesn't require artistic skill, and part of the fun is interpreting someone's drawings. It's a good way to get out of the regular grind and hear about each person's week.

SUPPLIES
- Paper
- Assorted pens, colored pencils, and markers

INSTRUCTIONS
1. Have each family member draw four pictures—one thing they did and three things they did not do that week.

2. Then each person passes their drawing to the left.

3. When you get another person's drawing, put your name by the image you think is a picture of something they did.

4. Keep passing your paper to the left until each player gets their drawing back. If you choose the correct activity on someone else's paper, give yourself five points. If someone guessed the wrong answer on your piece of paper, give yourself one point.

Let's Talk About It: You don't have to consider yourself an artist for this activity, and it's accessible to all ages. Guessing what someone has drawn can be part of the fun. How easy was it to interpret other people's drawings? Any surprises?

For Next Time: Another way to play this game is to draw four things you did do and one you didn't. Have each person guess which drawing is incorrect.

Would You Rather?

This game of questions for kids and adults reveals interesting and sometimes surprising things about your family. It can also make players think about what they value most. The questions can be silly, strange, and sometimes gross, but it's sure to bring your blended family together in a fun way.

INSTRUCTIONS

This activity entails reading a series of statements out loud and asking each person in the family which one they would rather do. Some sample questions are listed here. Have fun coming up with your own!

WOULD YOU RATHER:

1. Find a roach in your bed or a rat in the kitchen?

2. Eat a plate of broccoli or a plate of salad without dressing?

3. Go on a roller coaster that turns upside down or on a ride that spins really fast?

4. Live in a treehouse or a seaside cave?

5. Go potty in a bucket or in the woods?

6. Wear the same socks for a month or the same underwear for a week?

7. Spend a week in a submarine at the bottom of the ocean or at the International Space Station?

8. Drive to work in reverse or walk to work in heels?

9. That your best friend wins $100,000 or you win $25,000?

Let's Talk About It: **Which scenario did you enjoy most? What questions would you add to the list? Whose answer were you most surprised by?**

For Next Time: **Come up with your own scenarios!**

The Truth Is . . .

This activity generates lots of discussion and is a great way for a newly blended family to learn more about one another. As you uncover the truth by guessing how someone would answer the following questions, you find commonalities and differences among other family members—healing tensions that have formed and creating new bonds.

SUPPLIES
- Index cards
- Assorted pens, colored pencils, or markers

INSTRUCTIONS
1. You'll start this activity by creating a list of questions for the game and putting them on index cards. Here are some sample questions:

   My favorite thing to wear is _____.

   If I could choose anywhere to celebrate my birthday, it would be _____.

   The most expensive thing I recently purchased was _____.

   The chore I least like to do around the house is _____.

   My favorite teacher of all time is _____.

   If I could have an unusual animal for a pet, it would be _____.

   If I were an Olympic athlete, the sport I'd play would be _____.

   If I were a tree, I'd be _____.

   If I could go anywhere in the world, I'd go to _____.

   I could do _____ all day and not consider it a waste of time.

2. Decide who will be the "host" and pass out blank index cards to the other family members.

3. Each person will write their name on the index card before they begin.

4. The host will then draw a card from the stack of questions and read the question out loud.

5. The rest of the family members will write down how they think the host would answer the question. Meanwhile, the host writes their answer on the back of their card.

6. Once everyone is done writing the answer to the question, the host collects all the cards, including their own, and shuffles them together.

7. Then the host reads the question out loud as well as each answer that was given, keeping the answers anonymous.

8. Next, each participant votes on what they think the true answer is by writing it down on a new index card.

9. Players cannot vote for their own answer.

10. Players who write the correct answer get 10 points. Players who pick the answer from the list get 5 points, and players get a point anytime someone guesses their wrong answers.

Let's Talk About It: This is a fun way to see how well you know each person in your family. If you didn't know the answer, what was your strategy in writing the correct answer? Did anyone surprise you with their answers?

For Next Time: Some people play this game by making a "no duplicate" rule. If two or more players write the same answers, the host can choose one and return the others to their authors to try again.

Where Do You Stand?

In this activity, everyone will tell their own truth as they explain where they stand on an issue. This game invites families to listen, question, and debate as they broaden their own perspectives and learn about others'. In blended families, learning to listen and hear one another's opinions is of paramount importance for building trust and good communication.

SUPPLIES

- Paper
- Markers
- Painter's tape, rope, or any material that will mark lines

INSTRUCTIONS

1. You'll need to do several things to prepare for this activity:

   - Create signs that say "Agree" and "Disagree"
   - Come up with scenarios that are age appropriate for your family.

2. You'll hang one sign ("Agree") on one side of the room and the other sign ("Disagree") on the other side of the room. Stretch a line from one sign to the other. This could be a piece of rope, tape, etc.

3. When the room is set up, one person will read each statement out loud, and the rest of the family will decide where they stand on the issue. They can either walk to the "Agree" sign or the "Disagree sign" or position themselves anywhere in between. Standing somewhere along the line can indicate you are unsure of where you stand, or that you agree or disagree but have some reservations.

4. Once each person arrives at a spot on the continuum, the person who read the statement out loud asks each family member to explain where they stand on the issue and why.

HERE ARE SOME SAMPLE STATEMENTS:

- Honesty is the most important quality in a friend.

- Children should have limits on screen time.

- Tests are a good way to motivate a child in school.

- Playing a game is fun only when you win.

- Public transportation should be provided for free.

YOU CAN ALSO CREATE SCENARIOS TO READ ALOUD, LIKE THIS ONE:

Bennie has been struggling in school and is worried about an upcoming test. On the afternoon of the test, he finds out that his friend Tara has taken the test in the morning, and she remembers all the questions and the correct answers. She shares them with Bennie (who memorizes them as best he can) before he has to take his test. How strongly do you agree or disagree with Bennie's actions? How about what Tara did?

Let's Talk About It: This activity is a great way to hear what everyone thinks about important issues. Where did you and your family members stand on the statements and scenarios that were presented? Were you surprised to find out some of your family member's opinions on the topics that were discussed? Were there times that you stood alone on a spot on the line? What was that like?

For Next Time: This is a great opportunity for kids to think up their own scenarios. They could be based on real things that have happened to them or they can make them up. Depending on the age of your children, you can use current events that have taken place and discuss how politicians have handled them. Where do your family members stand on these current events?

The Danger of Stereotypes

This activity offers an opportunity to understand what stereotypes are, where they come from, and how they can lead to bias and discrimination. You'll have the opportunity to discuss the assumptions that people have made about you and the harm that stereotypes can cause. If you have a blended family that's made up of different cultures, races, and genders, this is a good way to understand each person's experience in the world and deepen your relationship with them as you learn about the danger of a single story.

SUPPLIES

- YouTube video of a TED Talk by the novelist Chimamanda Ngozi Adichie called "The Danger of a Single Story"

INSTRUCTIONS

1. In this activity, have an adult begin the conversation about stereotypes by asking members of the family the following questions (some are designed for younger members of the family and some questions everyone should answer).

2. For younger members of the family, start by asking: What do you know about the word *stereotype*—how would you define it?

3. Then when everyone has had a chance to respond, you can add to their understanding: A stereotype is a belief about someone based on the characteristics (either real or imagined) of a group they belong to. For example, all tall people are good basketball players, Indigenous people all live on reservations, and women are better cooks than men. Even a stereotype that seems positive has the danger of reducing someone to a single category or label and tells an incomplete or inaccurate story.

4. Stereotypes are, in part, how prejudice is formed. Yet people have a natural tendency to make patterns and predictions about

people. It is normal to group people according to similarities and differences, but it can have negative consequences.

THEN HAVE EACH PERSON IN THE FAMILY ANSWER:

- Has someone ever assumed something about you?

- Was it a positive assumption or a negative one?

- How did you respond?

5. Next, watch the TED Talk. After the video, have a conversation with your family. Here are some sample questions to discuss the video:

- What was Chimamanda Ngozi Adichie saying?

- Why do you think the talk is titled "The Danger of a Single Story"?

- What assumptions were made about Chimamanda Ngozi Adichie?

- What assumptions did she make about others?

- What did you learn about stereotypes?

Let's Talk About It: Using Chimamanda Ngozi Adichie's story as a jumping-off point is a great way to start a conversation about stereotypes in your family. Where do you think stereotypes come from? What are some stereotypes you have heard? What is harmful about stereotypes? In what ways do stereotypes lead to bias and discrimination? How can you challenge stereotypes?

For Next Time: For younger children, you can use a picture book to start a discussion about stereotypes, such as Dogs Don't Do Ballet by Anna Kemp and Sara Ogilvie. For older elementary and middle school aged children, Jesús Colón's story Little Things are Big can be read to discuss how stereotypes influenced a man's decision to help a woman with her stroller in a New York City subway station.

CHAPTER ELEVEN

Get Outside

F amilies are spending less time outdoors than ever before. Research shows that being in nature can reduce anxiety, depression, and stress—experiences that can be all too common in blended families. Some evidence even suggests that disconnection from nature—less green time—can exacerbate mental health issues. Although not all the activities in this chapter are nature related, they'll get your family outdoors. From Micro-Adventures (page 108) to an outdoor mural, the activities in this chapter will help lift everyone's mood.

Micro-Adventures

A Micro-Adventure is a short, low-cost or free adventure that is close to home. It's a great way to inspire moments of awe that can promote positive prosocial behavior and greater happiness. This activity helps blended families disrupt their normal routine, get out of the house or apartment, and appreciate their surroundings in a new way. Micro-Adventures are a good way to find great joy in a simple excursion.

SUPPLIES

- It all depends on your Micro-Adventure

INSTRUCTIONS

Here are some ideas for a short, inexpensive adventure that's close to home:

1. Take an evening bike ride or a hike in the dark. Don't forget snacks and water.

2. If you live near a big city, explore the tallest building or any building with a view. Take pictures from the top.

3. Ride a bus or a train to the last stop. Have lunch at the end of the line and then find your way home.

4. Find a climbable tree near you and make it a monthly micro-adventure to climb it. It doesn't matter how high you get. If able, adults should try to.

5. Find a place for an overnight that you've never been before.

Let's Talk About It: **What did you enjoy about the Micro-Adventure? Did you run into any challenges? What would you do next time?**

For Next Time: **Each week, come up with a new Micro-Adventure. Remember, they don't have to take long. They can happen after school, on the weekend, and even on a weeknight.**

Two Creative Ways to Have a Picnic

Picnics are a great way to get out of the house, lift everyone's spirits, and add a fun element to a regular routine. These two picnic spots will take you out of your normal routine and maybe even your typical breakfast. It might even inspire a new tradition for your family. The consistency of a shared tradition can ease transitions in a family dynamic.

SUPPLIES
- Picnic food
- Plates
- Napkins
- Utensils

INSTRUCTIONS

1. **Donuts at Dawn:** Okay, you don't have to start your picnic at 5:30 a.m. with donuts, but the idea is that you'll have breakfast with your family in a special place with a morning treat. This may mean a morning trip to the beach before the crowds arrive, or a special place in nature that the whole family enjoys. If you're not going too far, like your backyard, you may even want to let your children keep their pajamas on while they eat donuts in the yard.

2. **A Fort Picnic:** This picnic will take place in a fort that you and your family build. Especially fun for younger children, this activity requires some materials for a fort, such as an old sheet and outdoor chairs, or even a tent you put up at the park.

Let's Talk About It: **Did you discover a new place to have a picnic? How was it? Would you return?**

For Next Time: **Depending on the age of your children, have your child plan the whole picnic. What will you eat? Where will you go? Have the children lead the way and organize the outing.**

Water Balloon Relay

What's a hot day without water balloons? In this fun relay game, you'll partner with a family member to practice balance, precision, and strategy as you go from the starting line to the finish line without dropping your water balloon. Partner people who might not spend much time together to increase their connection through movement and laughter.

SUPPLIES

- Water balloons
- Cones, chalk, rope, or any material that will mark lines
- Laundry baskets or containers for catching water balloons (optional)

INSTRUCTIONS

1. The goal of this activity is for each pair of people to successfully move five water balloons from the starting line to the finish line, and then safely deposit them into a waiting bucket without bursting the balloons.

2. Divide your family into partners. If possible, you may want to partner people who are roughly the same height.

3. The starting and finish lines should be about 20 feet apart. It can be closer if there are younger family members. You can identify the starting and finish lines with cones, chalk, rope, or any material that will mark the beginning and the end.

4. Have each pair of people stand back-to-back at the starting line, with one person facing toward the finish line and one facing away.

5. Each pair will then place a water balloon between their backs, pushing slightly to create enough pressure to hold the balloon, but not so much that it bursts!

6. Once the balloon has been secured between their backs, the partners then link arms and stand at the starting line awaiting all pairs to be ready to go.

7. Someone counts to three and the partners are off—carefully but quickly carrying the water balloon between their backs!

8. Once the teams leave the starting line, they are not allowed to touch the water balloon with their hands.

9. Upon reaching the finish line, if successful in transporting an intact water balloon, the pair then works to carefully drop their water balloon into their waiting bucket without making it burst.

10. If a balloon bursts while en route to the waiting bucket, the pair must return to the starting line and retrieve another balloon and repeat the process.

11. When the teams have successfully carried a water balloon over the finish line and dropped their water balloon in a bucket, they must run back for another.

12. Whichever pair carries five water balloons successfully to the finish line wins (or whichever team successfully transfers the greatest number wins).

Let's Talk About It: Playing with water on a hot day is a good way to bring the whole family together. What strategy did you use to get the water balloons to the finish line? What was the most challenging aspect of this activity? What was it like working with your partner? If you could pick any partner, who would you pick?

For Next Time: There are many fun ways to play with water balloons! One of my favorites is the Laundry Basket Catch. Of course, any container will do. This can be played with two players or more. Each person or team stands away from one another and tries to throw and catch a water balloon using the laundry basket. Use a net if you have one. You get one point for a balloon that is caught and not dropped. Also, try bowling with water balloons. In this activity, you knock over plastic water bottles with water balloons.

Family Mural

Art is a great way to bring a blended family together. Even if someone in the family doesn't feel like an "artist," there are other roles to play while making a mural. Planning, execution, and celebration are all integral parts of this project, while creativity, teamwork, and problem-solving also come into play.

SUPPLIES

- Assorted pens, colored pencils, and markers
- Paper
- Chalk
- Primer (optional)
- Paints
- Paintbrushes (the size will depend on your design)
- Plastic lids or paper plates
- Plastic spoons
- Rags or paper towels

INSTRUCTIONS

1. Bring everyone in the family together via a family meeting or a conversation after dinner to start the planning process.

2. Bring pens and paper to the conversation as you brainstorm answers to the following questions:

- Where should the mural go? Do you have a backyard fence or outside wall that can house the mural?

- Do you want it to be visible to neighbors or other people?

- If you don't have a space yourself, maybe someone in the neighborhood would donate a fence or wall for a small mural.

- What should the focus of the mural be? What symbols or pictures will the mural include?

- Who would like to do which parts? You'll need someone to sketch the final ideas on the wall, someone to do the painting, someone to clear the space for the mural.

3. On a large piece of paper, sketch the ideas(s) you've come up with for the mural.

4. Then decide which family members will do the initial drawing in chalk on the fence or wall that you've chosen.

5. Once an outline is drawn in chalk, begin painting the designs.

6. If you're using a large wall or fence, you may want to use a primer first, but it's not essential.

7. Begin by mixing and creating the colors you want and then start painting!

8. When you're finished, don't forget to celebrate. You could do this by taking pictures and sending to friends and family or inviting friends and relatives over for a special snack and showing of the mural.

Let's Talk About It: Murals hold important stories in them. What does this mural say about your family? What story does it tell? How did your family work together to create the mural? What was your favorite part about making the mural? What did you learn about yourself and other family members in this process? How did you celebrate the completion of the mural? If you could do it again, what would you paint this time? Murals are also great conversation starters. Who could you invite over to celebrate your mural with?

For Next Time: Art changes how a space feels and how people experience that space. Is there a place in your neighborhood that could use a beautification project? If you like the idea of this project but don't have a space in or near your home to put up a mural, where else could you create one? What about your school, your local park, or other public place?

Fill the Bucket

In this activity, children learn that every drop of water counts. You can explain to younger children in the family that water is a precious resource around the world and that in some places, water sources are far from people's homes. In those places, people walk several miles a day to carry heavy loads of water for their families to drink. This is a great activity for blended families to collaborate and have some fun competition while remembering that water is a precious resource.

SUPPLIES

- Paper or plastic cups
- Scissors or knife
- Chalk, string, cones, or any material that will mark lines
- Buckets or other containers

INSTRUCTIONS

1. You'll need one paper or plastic cup for each person.

2. Use scissors or a knife to punch three to five small holes in each cup. Make sure you have the same number of holes and that they are roughly the same size and in the same place.

3. Then set up a starting line and a finish line using chalk, string, cones, or another indicator.

4. Each player (or team) will need two large containers—one bucket of water on the starting line full of water to fill your cup with, and one empty bucket at the finish line to pour your cup of water into.

5. Fill one of the buckets with water. That is the container you'll fill your cup from. Place the other bucket or container at the finish line.

6. When everyone is ready to begin, have each participant line up on the starting line next to their bucket with their cup in hand.

7. When you say, "go," each person will quickly fill their cup of water from the bucket and carry it to the bucket on the finish line. They will dump their cup of water—or what's left if it—in the empty bucket and head back to the water bucket to refill their cup again.

8. Each participant will continue to go back and forth with their cup until they have emptied the bucket of water on the starting line.

9. The person who ends up with the most water in the water collection bucket at the end wins the game.

Let's Talk About It: This activity takes speed, agility, and some strategy to get your cup quickly from one bucket to the other. How easy or difficult was it to transport water from a leaky cup? What challenges popped up along the way? What strategy worked well to carry the water? What would have made it more successful?

For Next Time: If you have enough people, try playing this game as a relay. Or create an obstacle course that you'll need to wade through as you transfer the water from one bucket to another. You can also try playing this game with sponges instead of cups. Dip a large sponge in the bucket, run back to the empty bucket, and wring your sponge out. The first person to empty the original bucket full of water and fill another one wins.

CHAPTER TWELVE

Build Trust

Trust is one of the cornerstones of a good relationship. In blended families, trust can take years to build and is easily eroded by jealousy, favoritism, and resentment. The activities in this chapter help family members work together, rely on one another for support, and appreciate the special qualities of each person in the family. Some activities call for blindfolds, increasing the challenge of the activity and the need for good communication, while other activities require supporting a partner or working as a team. Special Time (page 124) is an activity that you can do with each person in the family for the rest of their lives.

A Not-So-Perfect Square

This activity is a lot more difficult than it sounds! In this activity, you'll work together to create a square out of a long piece of rope. As you join forces, you'll build trust, collaboration, and good communication with your whole family.

SUPPLIES
- 1 long piece of rope (about 32 feet long)
- Blindfolds for each participant

INSTRUCTIONS

1. Explain to your family that you'll work together to make a square on the floor with a piece of rope—while blindfolded!

2. Make sure you're in a room or outdoor space that has a large enough workspace. One person should keep the rope with them.

3. Have each person tie a blindfold around their eyes.

4. When everyone is ready, the person with the rope will pass it to the other members of the family, making sure that each person has some of the rope.

5. Then you'll work together to create a large square on the floor or ground in front of you.

6. Once you think you've finished, take your blindfolds off and discuss the shape you've made.

Let's Talk About It: **How did it go? Were you successful? What was the communication like among your family? How did having a blindfold on affect your communication? What worked about your approach? What could you do differently next time? Did someone take a leadership role while constructing the square? Who was it?**

For Next Time: **Try making a different shape—a parallelogram, a rhombus, a triangle, or a circle.**

A Willow Tree in the Wind

Relax and let the wind (or rather, someone's hands) blow you from one family member to the next. This activity works best with a family of five or more. As you settle in and let the weight of your body be moved from one family member to the next, a trust is built.

INSTRUCTIONS

1. Decide who will be the willow tree first. The other family members will form an inward-facing circle around the willow tree.

2. Those family members who are creating the circle should stand in a spotting position, where each person puts one foot in front of the other and flexes their knees in order to balance. Stretch out your arms and lock your elbows, ready to catch the person in the middle.

3. The person who is the willow tree will stand in the middle of the circle, with their arms crossed over their chest and hands on their shoulders. They should keep their body straight and eyes closed.

4. The spotters should be standing shoulder to shoulder, creating a tight circle. With arms stretched out, they should be able to reach the person in the center of the circle.

5. The person in the middle of the circle will close their eyes and lean back and forth as other players gently push them until they fall.

6. Make sure each family member gets a turn in the center of the circle for a minute or two.

Let's Talk About It: **How comfortable did you feel as the willow tree? What would help you feel safer? At what times do you feel you need extra support in your life?**

The Hula-Hoop Challenge

If your child's Hula-Hoop days are over, this is a fun way to dust off that old toy and have fun with the whole family. This activity can be played inside on a rainy day or outside at the park after a picnic. It will test everyone's ability to maneuver a Hula-Hoop around the circle without dropping linked hands. You'll learn how to work together, collaborate, and problem-solve as you move the hoop around. You may even improve your flexibility and balance along the way! Though this takes a certain amount of agility, it's a good way for blended family members of various ages to appreciate one another's abilities and cheer them on.

SUPPLIES
- 1 or 2 Hula-Hoops

INSTRUCTIONS

1. Find a space large enough for everyone to form a circle. Explain that the goal of this activity is to pass the Hula-Hoop around the circle as quickly as you can without letting go of your teammate's hands.

2. Players form a circle, and one person puts the Hula-Hoop over their arm. Then everyone holds hands.

3. See how quickly you can pass the Hula-Hoop around the circle without letting go of your hands. This usually entails ducking your head so that the Hula-Hoop falls over your shoulders and drops toward your feet, then lifting it back up to your other arm so that the person next to you can grab it.

4. If anyone lets go of their partner's hands, you must start again.

5. When the Hula-Hoop gets back to the place it started, the challenge is complete.

6. When you've passed it around once, discuss what strategy you can use to get it around faster a second time.

Let's Talk About It: This activity takes a good plan and a lot of teamwork! What strategy was successful in getting the Hula-Hoop around the circle? What was the biggest challenge in this activity? Did your hands ever come unlinked? How difficult was it to use other parts of your body and not your hands? As you watched other family members pass the Hula-Hoop around the circle, did it give you good ideas when the hoop got to you? If you timed this activity, how long did it take? Can you beat your own record?

For Next Time: If you have a large family, you can divide into two teams and see who can get the Hula-Hoop around fastest. Another option with a large family, or when friends are over, is to form two lines facing one another. Pass one Hula-Hoop down each line, seeing who can get it to the end the fastest. And of course, there are many other games you can play with a Hula-Hoop. Try propping it against the wall or laying it on the floor and using it as a target for beanbags or water balloons. Have a roll-off. See how far each member of the family can roll the Hula-Hoop through a backyard, park, or other empty space. You can also use a Hula-Hoop to learn how to skip or improve your jump. Holding the Hula-Hoop with two hands in front of you, bring it down toward your feet and jump through it. Then bring it back over your head again and repeat.

Make It through the Minefield

There are no explosives in this activity, only household objects to avoid. To build trust and communication among family members, you'll help one another navigate a minefield of objects with a blindfold on. If the blindfolded person touches one of the objects in the minefield, they'll have to start again! Finding your way through a minefield takes good coordination and decision-making. Obstacle courses also require balance and patience and help people adjust to changing circumstances. A blended family can feel a little like an obstacle course in the early years. It's all about knowing how to navigate a changing environment.

SUPPLIES

- Household objects for obstacles, such as plastic containers, paper, toys, or pens
- Tape
- Blindfolds

INSTRUCTIONS

1. For this activity, you'll gather household objects to create a minefield. This could include plastic containers, paper, toys, pens, or other things you have around your home. Make sure they are small enough to ensure a safe game.

2. Choose a large enough open space in your home or outside for the minefield.

3. Decide where your starting and finish line will be. You can use tape or some other marker to indicate each line. They should be roughly 12 feet apart.

4. Gently lay out the objects for the minefield in between the start and finish line.

5. Divide your family into partners. Each pair will decide who will be the guide and who will be the one who will be blindfolded. The blindfolded person will not be allowed to talk. They'll have to listen carefully to the instructions of the guide but cannot ask questions.

6. The guide then navigates the blindfolded person through the obstacles.

7. The guide is allowed to talk and give directions, but not to touch the blindfolded person.

8. The goal is to get to the finish line without stepping on an obstacle. If the blindfolded person steps on an obstacle, they will need to return to the beginning and start again.

Let's Talk About It: In this activity, family members will practice clear communication while building trust and a sense of safety. What roles do trust and communication play in this activity? For the person who was blindfolded, what was frustrating about not being able to talk or see? If you had to start again because you stepped on an obstacle, what would have helped you avoid that in the future? What did you learn about trust and communication that you can apply to other areas of your life?

For Next Time: On a hot day, create an outside water-themed obstacle course that includes throwing water balloons in buckets, jumping over pool noodles, or running through sprinklers. Or you could increase the difficulty and have blindfolded players balance an egg on a spoon as they walk through the minefield!

Special Time

One of the best ways to build trust and safety in relationships in blended families is through one-on-one time. This activity addresses many of the issues that arise in blended families. When children feel jealous, left out, or in need of attention, Special Time comes to the rescue. Many blended families hope to be one big happy family right away. But doing so can take time to achieve, sometimes even years. Spending more time on building individual relationships in a blended family can pay off down the road. Children in blended families can feel like they have no control over the decisions that are made. Special Time helps a child who goes from one house to the other feel like they have a say in how things go. It's an important way to build trust, understanding, and love in a blended family.

INSTRUCTIONS

This activity is usually done with one adult and one child, but it could be done with two adults and one child and could even be done with two adults. This is how it works:

1. The adult decides on the amount of time. If you're doing special time with a young child, 15 to 20 minutes is sufficient; even 10 minutes can work well with a young child.

2. Start by telling your child you'll do whatever they want to do or play whatever they want to play—within the limits of safety and reason.

3. Put away your phone and any other distractions and make sure others in the family are occupied or taken care of if they are small.

4. Set a timer and enjoy uninterrupted time with your child or stepchild.

5. Each child in the family should get about an hour of Special Time each week.

Let's Talk About It: **Special Time is different than other types of one-on-one time because it is child led. The key to this activity is that the child (or person who is receiving Special Time) gets to tell you exactly what they want to do or play. For the person receiving Special Time—what was it like? What did you enjoy about it? What would you plan for next time? Is there anything your parent or stepparent could have done differently? Adults can consider what it was like themselves. Did you get bored? Was it fun to spend that time with your child or stepchild?**

For Next Time: **It's a good idea to start small with Special Time—even 10 to 15 minutes can go a long way with a young child. As time goes on, you can increase the increments of Special Time. This activity looks different at every age and stage. For younger children, it may consist of a short 10-minute play session, while for an older child it might entail leaving the house for a short amount of time. Although the child gets to choose the activity, the adult determines how much time and money can be spent during Special Time.**

CHAPTER THIRTEEN

Love One Another

You are wired for love. But it's not always easy to show it. In this chapter, there are a variety of suggestions for how to express your love and care for your family members. In blended families, when children are not sure where they stand or how much they are loved, these activities will help them know that they are deeply cared for. There are also suggestions here that will help couples feel closer, and ones that will help siblings appreciate one another. Get ready to shower some love on your family and receive a few hugs in the process.

Create Your Own Family Holiday

Holidays in any family can be tense, but in blended families they can be especially difficult. Missing loved ones, feeling left out, and disappointment can all surface for both children and parents in blended families. You may want to consider creating your own family holiday. It could be during traditional holiday time or any other month of the year. You don't have to wait for a big event, a milestone, or a traditional holiday. You can celebrate with a gift, a special meal, or an outing any time of the year!

INSTRUCTIONS

1. Work as a family to develop a holiday theme or topic and choose what day you want to celebrate.

2. Decide on a name for your holiday.

3. Come up with an activity for your holiday. This could include an excursion your family enjoys, a favorite meal, and gifts.

4. Is it just for your family or will you invite friends and relatives?

5. Will you have music and dancing?

6. If you have young children, they may want to make special decorations.

Let's Talk About It: **What did you do for your new family holiday? What would you do differently next time? What ways of celebrating make you feel special?**

For Next Time: **Find reasons to celebrate each member of the family. As you celebrate small things like getting your braces off, the end of a sports season, or completing a project, the celebrations compound, and you find more things to celebrate, which expands positive feelings in the family. You're not just celebrating learning how to ride a bike or figuring out a tough math problem—you're celebrating *you*. Celebrating each person in a blended family helps everyone feel important, special, and loved.**

Family Manifesto

This activity is a great way to discuss and display your family values and beliefs. It shows children in a blended family they are a part of something special and gives everyone a sense of belonging and connection. A manifesto highlights what families love and what they stand for.

SUPPLIES

- Paper
- Assorted pens, colored pencils, and markers
- Poster board

INSTRUCTIONS

1. Explain what a manifesto is—a graphic that explains who you are as a family, your core values, and the things that are important to you.

2. Take notes as you brainstorm the following questions.

- What is important to your family?
- What does your family believe in?
- What is culturally important to your family?
- What are some of your favorite family activities?
- How do we want to treat one another and others outside this household?

3. Thinking about what you brainstormed, use one or all of the following sentence starters:

   "We are a family that ..."

   "In our house, we ..."

   "We believe ..."

4. For example, "In our house, we love unconditionally, laugh a lot, play soccer, and dream big."

Continued »

5. Create a graphic representation of your ideas. This could be a small or large poster, depending on what size paper you have.

6. Have someone in the family write what you've come up with while others make drawings and symbols to decorate the poster.

7. Decide where you'd like to display it in your home.

Let's Talk About It: **What did you discover about your family by doing this activity? What do you love most about your family? What types of values did you agree on? These questions can generate insights on what different family members think is important, which can be helpful in avoiding conflicts and improving communication.**

For Next Time: **As time passes and children get older, you may want to update the manifesto. You can even make this an annual tradition. It reinforces a valuable lesson about growth and demonstrates the need for flexibility, which is crucial in a blended family that may have competing priorities at times.**

Listening with Love—Responding to Big Feelings

One of the most profound ways to show your love for another person is through listening. When a person feels heard, they feel safe, loved, and understood. When a parent or stepparent listens to an upset child without dismissing their feelings, the child can release stored emotions and be more compassionate and cooperative on the other side. When you deeply listen, without judging or ridiculing the child's experience, you create an unshakable bond with them.

INSTRUCTIONS

You may not always know what to say and do when your children are upset. In this activity, you'll practice listening with a partner or a friend. Through role-playing, you'll listen and respond to a child in a way that helps them heal. In this kind of listening, it's best if the listener does more listening than talking.

1. Have one person play the role of the child and the other person play the adult.

2. Think of a common scenario that occurs with your child that causes conflict between the two of you.

3. Have the person playing the child reenact the situation with the same words, feelings, and actions as the child would.

4. The adult will try listening with empathy and understanding. Instead of yelling, shaming, or speaking through clenched teeth, try some of the following phrases. If a boundary needs to be set, try setting limits with some of these expressions:

Continued »

Listening with Love—Responding to Big Feelings continued

INSTEAD OF SAYING:

- Don't worry.

- There's nothing to be afraid of.

- Calm down.

- You are so sensitive.

- It's not a big deal.

TRY:

- I know this is hard. It won't always be this way.

- I want to hear all about it.

- I don't want to leave you alone when you're feeling this way.

- Let's look at your knee and see what happened.

IF A BOUNDARY NEEDS TO BE SET, INSTEAD OF SAYING:

- Stop it! Enough!

- That's it. We're leaving!

- Don't be mad.

- Don't cry.

TRY:

- I'm not upset with you, but I do have to stop you.

- That isn't yours. It's time to give it back.

- I know you don't want to leave, but it's time to go.

Let's Talk About It: **When you listen with empathy and understanding, rather than anger or the intention to fix the problem, you open a new path for healing and hope. What did you notice as you listened in this way? What worked, and what didn't? What would you do differently next time? What was it like playing the role of the child?**

For Next Time: **Try listening to your partner with empathy and compassion, but without interjecting with advice. It can be helpful and satisfying to have someone just listen, empathize, and paraphrase our experience rather than try to solve a problem.**

The Power of Rituals

Even the smallest of rituals will leave lasting memories in a family. Rituals give family members a sense of identity and belonging—two things that can feel lacking in blended families. They can also transfer family history, culture, and values from one generation to the next or from one part of your blended family to the other. Rituals help family members understand what is important to the family and lets them know they are a part of something special. Traditions often help children in a blended family have a sense of security, as rituals are consistent and predictable.

SUPPLIES
* Supplies will vary

INSTRUCTIONS
Family rituals don't have to cost much, and they certainly don't have to be a big family vacation somewhere far away. Some require creativity and planning, while others are so simple that they may not even feel like rituals. There are many activities in this book that you can consider doing with your family on a regular basis. Remember to develop rituals you know you can stick to and won't abandon after a week or a month. Consistency is key to making something a ritual.

CONSIDER SOME OF THE FOLLOWING:

A Family Vision Board	(page 7)
The Family Meeting	(page 17)
Gratitude Time	(page 31)
Dinner Picnic	(page 48)
Collecting Memories	(page 60)
A Letter to Self	(page 64)
Looking Forward to the Future	(page 68)

Continued »

The Power of Rituals continued

Let's Talk About It: **For children who go between two homes, rituals help them develop a sense of security and stability. Rituals help create memories, increase connections between family members, and acknowledge cycles of time. When a ritual is absent or delayed—a missed graduation, or a birthday gone unmarked— it can be disappointing at the least and disorienting and destabilizing at the worst. What were some of your favorite rituals growing up? What rituals would you like to see in your family now? Which rituals do your children enjoy the most? What do they suggest you do more often?**

For Next Time: **Children are never too old for rituals. If things you did when the kids were toddlers embarrass or bore them now, find a new ritual that they enjoy. This may be watching their favorite TV show together on the weekend or taking them and their friends out to lunch once a month.**

5 Ways to Love Your Family and Yourself

Love notes, joy jars, and even apologies are wonderful ways to express your love for someone else. In this section, there are five activities or acts of love that show your family members how much you care. Stepchildren are not always sure where they stand in a blended family, so for a stepparent to choose one of the following gestures is especially meaningful.

SUPPLIES
- Supplies will vary

INSTRUCTIONS
SCHEDULE A LOVE BLAST
A Love Blast is like an extended Special Time (page 124). When you do a Love Blast, you take an excursion or short trip with another person in the family. The key is that the other person gets to choose where you go and what you do, within limits of expense and distance. You may not be able to do a Love Blast with each family member on a regular basis, but you can look at the calendar for the year and make sure each person gets their special afternoon or overnight at least once during that time.

LEAVE LOVE NOTES
A simple sticky note can do wonders for the relationships in your family. You can leave a love note in someone's lunch, in their favorite notebook, on their computer, or even under their bedroom door if things have gone awry. Love notes can be any affirmative statement about the other person. Maybe it's "I can't wait to see you when you get home," "I love your laughter," or "Good luck on the test, you're the best!"

Continued »

EXERCISE THE POWER OF APOLOGY

A heartfelt apology creates a powerful path to repair. When you apologize for something you've said or done, you tell the other person you understand that they are hurt and that you've made a mistake. You take responsibility and create a space for the other person to feel heard and to heal. Saying you're sorry is an important part of the language of love.

REMEMBER TO LOVE YOU!

You'll have little left to give if you're not loving yourself on a regular basis. Whatever self-care looks like for you, it's crucial to make time for it. When we take time out during the day or the week for ourselves—whether it's 10 minutes of meditation or coffee with a friend—we are modeling self-care for the whole family. You not only send a message that your needs are important, but you also signal to others that they should do the same.

JOY JAR

Another way to express your love to children is by creating a Joy Jar. If someone in the family is having a hard time or you're celebrating a milestone, find a jar or a bag and gather things you'll know they'll enjoy. You can stuff a joy jar with art supplies, plastic animals, sweet treats, or their favorite items.

Let's Talk About It: Love is expressed not only through words and actions, but also with delight in your eyes. Sometimes that light grows dim because you are tired, frustrated, or distracted. When that's the case, try some of the things in this activity and notice what happens. How did your child or partner respond when you left a love note or made an apology? What are some other ways you can show your love for someone?

For Next Time: Try coming up with your own list of activities to do as a family. After you've tried one activity, keep going!

CHAPTER FOURTEEN

Activities for Hard Times

H ard times come to all families, but there are healthy ways to weather the storm. This chapter invites you to laugh, breathe, move, manipulate DIY Theraputty (page 141), take therapeutic Brain Breaks (page 142), and try Tapping for Rapid Relief (page 146). Whether you're in the heat of a conflict or looking for ideas on how to maintain a peaceful home over the long haul, you'll find them here. While a stepchild's anger or stubbornness can be particularly aggravating for a stepparent, or an argument with an ex can affect the mood of an outing, blended families bring with them their own challenges. The activities in this chapter can be used when you're losing your cool or if you need a regular practice of relaxation.

Laughter Heals

Laughter can be the healing balm that blended families need in hard times. In 1976, Norman Cousins wrote *Anatomy of an Illness (as Perceived by the Patient)* in which he chronicled his recovery from a crippling autoimmune arthritis by taking large doses of vitamin C and laughing—a lot. While lying in the hospital, he realized that 10 minutes of deep laughter would give him 2 hours of pain relief. Laughter increases mood-elevating endorphins, reduces stress hormones, and relaxes the body. Laughter helps members of a blended family enjoy their time together and feel more compassionate toward one another.

INSTRUCTIONS

Norman Cousins watched old reruns of *Candid Camera* and Marx Brothers movies to incite laughter, but this activity generates giggles through physical effort.

1. Gather your family together and have everyone stand with their knees slightly bent.

2. Loosen your arms and begin by forcing laughter up from your belly.

3. Let out whatever sounds come as you try to laugh. This may be giggles, grunts, full-belly laughter, or snorting.

Let's Talk About It: **We know that laughter is contagious. Research has shown that when you hear laughter, the area in your brain that controls smiling and giggling is activated as you prepare to mirror someone else's emotions. Did other people make you laugh in this activity? What normally makes you laugh, and how can you share more laughter in your family?**

For Next Time: **Warm up by watching something funny together or sharing hilarious stories and jokes.**

DIY Theraputty

Whether you tap your foot, twirl your hair, or crack your knuckles, most people fidget. And it turns out that intentional fidgeting is good for you. Research indicates that fidgeting helps you increase your focus and reduces anxiety. Intentional fidgeting is a popular academic support for children with ADHD and sensory processing difficulties, but even adults enjoy the benefits of this activity.

SUPPLIES

- 2 medium-size bowls
- Plastic spoon or wooden stick
- 1 cup glue
- 1 cup water
- Food coloring
- ½ cup warm water
- 1 teaspoon borax

INSTRUCTIONS

1. In a medium bowl, stir together the glue and 1 cup of water.

2. Mix in food coloring to give your Theraputty some pizazz.

3. In a separate bowl, mix ½ cup of warm water and borax. Mix until the borax is dissolved. If it doesn't dissolve completely, it should in the next step.

4. Slowly pour the borax mixture into the glue mixture and stir well.

5. Knead the putty with your hands until it is no longer sticky.

6. Remove any excess water from the putty and the bowl.

7. Store in an airtight container.

Let's Talk About It: Once you make the Theraputty, discuss when and where you can use it. If someone in the family feels nervous or anxious, it's a good time to get out the Theraputty. If someone has a video meeting, Theraputty can be the anchor that's needed on a stressful call. Where else can you use it?

For Next Time: There are a variety of things you can do with Theraputty. With younger kids, try making numbers, animals, or letters with the putty.

Brain Breaks

Although some teachers have incorporated brain breaks into their curriculum, they're not just for classrooms. Brain Breaks are small mental breaks that can improve productivity, increase your energy, help you relax, and enhance your creativity. When someone in the family is upset, small movement breaks can help shake up a tense atmosphere. Brain Breaks allow you to stop what you're doing, control angry impulses, and be more thoughtful about your next steps.

SUPPLIES
* Die

INSTRUCTIONS
When someone needs a brain break, roll a die and refer to the following suggestions. Try the brain break that corresponds to the number rolled.

1 OR 4:
THE SHOULDER PULL
1. Start by putting your right hand on your left shoulder and drag your hand down diagonally across your chest.

2. Place your left hand on your right shoulder and drag your left hand across your chest diagonally to your waist.

3. Do this at least twice on each side.

2 OR 5:
THE CROSS CRAWL
1. In a standing or seated position, bring your left leg up while bending your knee and slap your right hand on your left knee as it's coming up.

2. Repeat for the other side.

3. Raise your right leg by bending your right knee, and cross your left arm over and touch your right knee.

4. Keep alternating sides in a continuous motion at least 10 times.

3 OR 6:
THE CAT/COW POSE

1. Begin on all fours. Make sure your shoulders are over your wrists and your hips are over your knees.

2. Look straight ahead, or if you can, look up at the sky, arch your back, and tuck your tailbone ("cat").

3. Let your head fall between your arms and tuck in your chest and chin ("cow").

4. Alternate between the two positions, the cat and the cow.

Brain Breaks work well in a variety of situations. Turn to a brain break when your child throws down their pencil in frustration and wants to quit, or when a sibling dispute has gone too far. When a parent is about to lose it, Brain Breaks are a refuge before the storm. They're also a fun way to start the morning and can be turned into a morning routine. When a child is anxious or upset before school, a playdate, or a doctor's appointment, a Brain Break moves the body and releases the fear or anxiety that builds before an event.

Let's Talk About It: Brain Breaks not only help reduce tension and anxiety, but they also help you focus and be more productive. Which was your favorite Brain Break? What did you notice after doing it? Was there a change in how you felt? Was there one Brain Break that was more difficult than the others?

For Next Time: What Brain Break would you add to the list? Try coming up with your own activities and adding them to the routine. It can be helpful to talk to family members individually about what works for them. Pretty soon you'll have a list that's tailored to your family's needs and can benefit everyone.

Soft Belly Breaths

A regular practice of meditation helps you quiet the agitation that comes with complex family dynamics. In addition to the physical benefits of meditation, such as reducing high blood pressure and promoting the growth of new brain tissue, meditation also helps you develop self-awareness, better judgment, and greater compassion. In short, meditation promotes hope—a key ingredient to a happy, blended family.

INSTRUCTIONS

The Soft Belly Breath is a type of concentrative meditation in which you focus on the breath and the words *soft belly*. This can be a great family relaxation practice before bed to ensure good sleep, or a fun way to spend a few minutes together on the weekend.

1. Bring your family together and let them know you're going to practice a breathing exercise.

2. Set up the space you're in so it's conducive to meditation. This may mean putting some flowers in the room, dimming the lights, and making sure there are comfortable places for each person to sit or lie.

3. Have everyone get into a comfortable sitting or lying position.

4. Close your eyes or focus them gently on the ground beneath you.

5. Become aware of your breath. Breathing in through your nose and out through your mouth, make sure your breaths are slow and deep.

6. On the inhale, your belly will expand. On the exhale, your belly will gently drop down as your belly button pulls in toward your backbone.

7. Continue in this pattern for 10 to 12 minutes. When you're just starting the meditation, you can do shorter stints—even a few minutes makes a difference. Eventually, you may want to build up to 15 minutes.

Let's Talk About It: **When you go into a meditative state, you often have a variety of thoughts, feelings, and emotions. Notice those thoughts or images and return your concentration to your breath. Was it easy or difficult to stay in a meditative state for 10 minutes? What thoughts came up when you were meditating? If you were distracted by your thoughts, were you able to get back to your breath?**

For Next Time: **There are hundreds of other types of meditations to do. For children or beginners, it can be helpful to listen to a recorded meditation. Depending on the age of your children, you may want to listen to a recording of James S. Gordon at the Center for Mind-Body Medicine as he leads you through the soft belly meditation. Or choose from over 2,000 meditation apps on the internet. Some popular relaxation apps include Headspace, Calm, and Simple Habit. When you have a little extra time, set up a spa night that starts with a soothing bath and massage and ends with a meditation. Many people find that meditation helps them sleep better. Developing a family meditation practice before bed can help you relax and let go of any stress or worries from the day.**

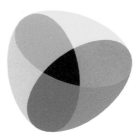

Tapping for Rapid Relief

The Emotional Freedom Technique (EFT), more typically referred to as "tapping," is a fast and efficient way to work through the many emotions that can surface in a blended family. Tapping helps reduce emotional tension and even physical pain. As we focus on our bodies and our emotions, we become more mindful of the upset or illness. And as you speak the words or allow the tears, anger, or worry to emerge, you let it out of your system so that you can relax again and remember that you love your family.

INSTRUCTIONS

1. Explain to your family that when they're feeling upset, these negative emotions can get trapped in their bodies and make them more tense or afraid. Rather than holding on to these emotions, it is healthier to let them out. One way to do that is through tapping.

2. Rooted in the ancient practice of acupuncture, tapping is done along your body's meridians. Meridians are known as pathways of energy. When someone taps along the meridian lines, their brain receives a signal that it is safe to relax and be calm. Studies have shown that tapping reduces the stress hormone cortisol.

3. Think of something that has angered or upset you; you can even speak it aloud. As you do this, use your fingers to tap on the points listed in step 4 for 3 to 5 minutes. The amount of time you tap will be guided by the intensity of the feeling. Some issues will take longer to clear than others.

4. Using the following tapping points, let your thoughts and emotions come to the surface as you speak, cry, laugh, yawn, or whatever wants to come out. You'll notice your body starting to relax as you let go of difficult feelings that were festering.

- The top of your head
- In between your eyebrows
- The side of your eye
- Under your nose
- Under your mouth
- On your collarbone
- Under your arm, a few inches beneath your armpit

5. Use a SUDS (Subjective Units of Distress) scale to measure the intensity of the issue. The SUDS scale works on a scale from 1 to 10—With "1" being no feeling at all and "10" being extremely intense. As you tap, check in with how you are feeling about your issue using the SUDS scale. As you tap, does the intensity lower? If not, keep tapping and releasing feelings.

6. Although you start with the negative feelings in tapping, you also want to tap on the positive ones as well. After 5 to 10 minutes of tapping, start saying affirmations aloud to yourself. Those statements might include: "I am grateful for every member of my family," "I am an amazing parent and partner," or "I am always learning from my mistakes."

Let's Talk About It: Most parents in blended families—in all families for that matter—experience multiple triggers a day. These are good things to tap on. What has happened lately or in the past that you could tap on and release? What was it like to try tapping? How did you feel when you were done tapping? What was your SUDS score?

For Next Time: For young children, you can make tapping fun by calling each point a "magic button." Or give the tapping points names like the "monkey spot" for the top of the head or the "gorilla spot" for the collarbone. You can also ask your child if you can tap on them. For example, if they are having trouble sleeping, ask them if you can go through their tapping points as they say what's on their mind.

CHAPTER FIFTEEN

Bridging the Divide through Technology

Technology is one of the great connectors. Although meaningful relationships cannot be replaced with technology, you can certainly enhance them through the digital world. The activities in this chapter encourage meaningful connections and time together. Whether you are listening to calypso on a dancing app (page 151), feeling warm and fuzzy as you watch puppies sleeping on a webcam (page 154), or creating a stop-motion extravaganza (page 152), you'll experiment with creative ways to connect and enjoy one another's company. Plus, technology can help family members (especially siblings and stepsiblings) stay connected when they aren't together in the same house.

Welcome to Their Tech World

I invite you to put aside any frustration, judgmental feelings, or worry that your kids have been online too much, and let them guide you through their digital world. When a child shares their favorite games or videos with you, you can appreciate who they are and what lights them up. When we let them teach us something new on the internet, it reverses the power dynamic and builds their self-esteem.

INSTRUCTIONS

Here are some ways to connect and collaborate online with your kids:

1. Let them take you on a tour of their favorite social media app.

2. Have them help you troubleshoot a tech problem you're having.

3. Join them in their latest video game.

4. Snuggle up with them watching their favorite TV show.

Remember to stay engaged and ask questions! Don't tune out on your phone while they're trying to share a video or give up on a game after just a few minutes.

Let's Talk About It: **The key to doing this kind of activity is to let your child be in charge. Have them pick the online activity and then let them steer. What did you learn about your child? Was it difficult to pay attention? Or did you find it more enjoyable than you thought?**

For Next Time: **You can also use the internet to look up places where family members grew up or share pictures or videos of your kids when they were little. If there are older children in the family, texting fun pictures, memes, or love notes is a good way to stay connected to children who have two homes.**

Digital Dancing!

It's time to get your groove on! And if that sounds awkward, that's half the fun. Dancing is a great way to bring everyone together. Dancing helps your body release endorphins, improves your mood, and can alleviate anxiety and depression. Don't be surprised if your experiment with the digital world of dance leads to laughter! Family dance is a good way to shed some embarrassment. If your children are older, you could be the healthy butt of a joke, but laughing at you can help children feel closer and more connected to you and relieve some tension, too. Just don't take it too seriously!

SUPPLIES
• Smartphone or tablet

INSTRUCTIONS
You need a dance app like Just Dance Now to start. With these apps you can choose a dance routine for any skill level. Set aside a weeknight to do a dance party, fire up the app of your choice, and get funky as a family.

Let's Talk About It: **No matter how good or bad you are at dancing, moving your body creatively with your family helps you enjoy their company more. Did you learn new moves? How did it go for everyone?**

For Next Time: **If you have older kids, learn a dance move on TikTok with them. Now that many dance studios have classes online, find your favorite family-friendly dance class on Zoom, turn off the camera if you're shy, and have a family groove night.**

Create a Stop-Motion Movie on Your Phone

If your family is curious about how moviemaking happens, creating a stop-motion video is a good way to dip your toes into the world of filmmaking. Creating a stop-motion film activates your iteration and problem-solving skills and is an opportunity for families to plan and project manage together. There are many kinds of stop-motion animation films. Younger children may want to use toys or building bricks as the centerpiece of their film, while older kids can make clay characters and paper cutouts, design illustrations, or gather found objects to create their stop-motion scenes.

SUPPLIES

- Props (toys, clay, puppets, etc.)
- White foam tri-fold presentation board (optional)
- Table
- Smartphone or tablet
- Stop-motion video app (see Resources on page 162)
- Tripod or stand to keep your device steady

INSTRUCTIONS

1. Designate a small space in your home that is quiet and won't be disturbed. You may end up leaving your materials there for several hours or even a few days, so you'll want to choose a place that is not in the way.

2. Decide what your stop-motion film will be about and what objects you'll use. For the first one, I suggest experimenting with one to two objects. Even though you may have a great idea for a story, you'll want to experiment with the technology and the process before you make the final cut.

3. If you're using a presentation board, set that up in your designated space. Otherwise, you can create your set by putting paper down on a table and using a wall for the background.

4. Install your app, then attach your device to a tripod or stand. If you're shaky while shooting, the movie might appear jumpy or lack continuity.

5. Shoot your movie. Follow the instructions on your app (they're all a little different) and remember some basics. Since you'll be taking one picture at a time but potentially dozens of pictures for the film, remember to move your props only small amounts between shots for smoother effects. Also keep the set clean so no random objects jump in or out of shots.

Let's Talk About It: **Creating a stop-motion film takes time and lots of patience. What was your favorite part of the process? What was the most challenging part? What other scenes and stories could you create?**

For Next Time: **Once everyone gets the hang of creating a stop-motion film, you can create more complicated scenes and stories by using a storyboard—a graphic representation of how your video will unfold. A storyboard is a great way to see what everyone is thinking and helps outline a more complex story.**

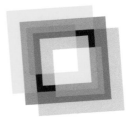

Animal Webcam

Watching animals helps with stress—a lot! You no longer have to travel to the wilderness or the Humane Society to see your favorite animals. Whether it's Alaskan brown bears catching salmon or a pile of sleeping puppies, webcams can be entertaining and relaxing. They can also help you hone your observation skills and gain knowledge about animals in a unique way. Animal Webcam is a great way for blended families to bond around a favorite furry creature or learn more about animals in the wild.

SUPPLIES
* Smartphone, tablet, or laptop

INSTRUCTIONS

Once you start down the animal webcam path, you'll be surprised at how many amazing, fuzzy (and not-so-fuzzy) creatures there are online. From South Africa to Southern California, there are hundreds of animal webcams to choose from. Consider starting with the following:

The Monterey Bay Aquarium webcams: MontereyBayAquarium.org/animals/live-cams

A multimedia organization that creates documentary films and operates live cams around the world: Explore.org

The San Diego Zoo webcams: Zoo.SanDiegoZoo.org/live-cams

A global network of over 1,800 livestreaming webcams: HDOnTap.com

The Dublin Zoo webcams: DublinZoo.ie/animals/animal-webcams

A webcam of the Djuma Waterhole in the Djuma Private Game Reserve: Djuma.com/djuma-waterhole

- Some webcams are more exciting than others. While you might be waiting for hours for a panda to lumber into view on one live feed, others have more action. The time of year will dictate the best times to watch webcams in nature. For example, July and September are good months to catch brown bears feasting on salmon in the streams of Katmai National Park in Alaska, while February to June is the best time to watch an eagle bringing food to its new offspring.

Let's Talk About It: You can learn a lot by watching an animal in their natural habitat. What's something new you learned from Animal Webcam? What questions came up during or after your viewing? If you were watching an animal over a period of days or weeks, what changed? Was anything introduced to the environment that was new? What surprised you about the animals you watched? What kinds of animal families did you find online? Who were their caretakers?

For Next Time: Viewing animals on a live feed in their natural habitat, rather than in person, can impact environmental conservation by keeping crowds away from popular spots. If you have family members that are animal enthusiasts, you could turn this activity into a conservation initiative. Organize an online fundraiser for your favorite wild animal by preparing a Zoom presentation that includes a viewing of the live feed, fun facts, and a pitch for donations. Or visit the Wild Animal Sanctuary Facebook page, where you can set up your own fundraising site. You might have a child who is eager to learn even more about the animal. Check out books from the library or do some extra research online. You can also have your child fill out an observation sheet. There are many animal webcam observation sheets online that have the observer draw the biome the animal lives in, describe what the animal is doing at the time of observation, and what was happening around it.

A Digital Newsletter

A Digital Newsletter is a good way to inform people of your family's comings and goings over the last year. It also helps members of a blended family who may feel left out or unseen to have a creative voice and be heard. It gives each person an important role that can highlight their strengths, whether it's writing, design or layout. Younger children can enjoy being interviewed by an older family member or drawing something for the newsletter, while older kids can help with the digital production. A newsletter acknowledges that each person in the family is important.

SUPPLIES

- Paper
- Assorted pens, colored pencils, and markers
- A website such as Canva for newsletter templates (see Resources page 161)

INSTRUCTIONS

1. First, bring your family together and decide who the audience is. Is it a small group of family members outside your immediate family, or is it for a larger group of friends and family? Knowing your audience will inform what you want to include.

2. Decide if there will be a theme to the newsletter or if it's just a recap of the year's events.

3. Naming the newsletter will give it a fun twist—the McAlister Musings or the Blumenthal Bulletin.

4. Decide who will work on which aspect of the newsletter. Younger children may want to use colored pencils and markers to create drawings. Or perhaps an adult can interview children and include quotes from the interview. Older children can have fun with graphic design and writing.

5. What topics do you want to cover in your newsletter? Engagements, births, weddings, birthdays, big moves, and career changes are always good options. But your newsletter doesn't have to be just announcements. Here are some other things to consider:

- Interview a grandparent or other relative and share a few of their memories in your newsletter.

- Include a poem or piece of art that the kids made last year.

- Add baby photos of your family and ask friends and family to guess who they are.

- Share a recent recipe that was a big hit in your family.

- Showcase a family member's new website.

6. Once you've completed a draft of your content, decide on the layout. Word has plenty of newsletter templates, or you may want to go with a free graphic design platform such as Canva.com.

7. Once you've given your newsletter a quick edit, it's ready to go! You can send it via email as a Word doc or PDF, or sites like Canva.com give you the option of downloading it in a variety of formats.

Let's Talk About It: What was your favorite part about creating a newsletter? Did you learn anything new about your family or relatives? What would you do differently next time?

For Next Time: Online newsletters are environmentally friendly and cheaper to send, but snail mail has a certain charm some relatives may like. If your family is enjoying the newsletter project, maybe it's time to create a family blog to celebrate accomplishments, acknowledge challenges, and keep everyone up to date on last year's events. And don't hesitate to stretch outside your creative comfort zone. One family I know wrote a newsletter from the perspective of their family dog!

A FINAL NOTE

Research suggests that quality family bonding leads to better mental health outcomes. As common as it is to schedule work meetings, doctor's appointments, or tutoring sessions, rarely as parents do you plan family connection time. When you put connection time on the calendar and make it a priority each week, you improve the odds.

The activities in this book help you come together, learn, communicate, build trust and understanding, appreciate, and encourage one another. Whether you're creating a vision board, drawing a family portrait, or acting out a scene from your imagination, these activities help you reimagine the future, spark reflective dialogue, and remind each person in the family that their very presence is important and that they belong.

As you filled water balloons, had family meetings, or explored your neighborhood through a scavenger hunt, what did you notice? Which activities did you enjoy most? What challenges popped up?

Conflicts are bound to emerge when families come together. Many of the activities in this book resolve tension through play, laughter, listening, empathy, and understanding. What have you noticed about conflict and connection in your family? Which activities would you turn to in the future to help you resolve the challenges that emerge as you come together with stepchildren, partners, and stepparents?

The activities in this book remind families that with a little effort and focused attention, you can have richer, more meaningful relationships with everyone in your blended family. How can you maintain closeness and connection in your family over the coming weeks and years?

RESOURCES

Books

Listen: Five Simple Tools to Meet Your Everyday Parenting Challenges **by Patty Wipfler and Tosha Schore** A great parenting resource that includes real-life stories of how to implement tools that help parents build connection and resolve some of their biggest parenting challenges.

Peaceful Parent, Happy Kids **by Laura Markham** This book is full of practical tools that help parents understand their own emotions as well as those of their children. You'll also discover what to say and do during a tantrum, a power struggle, and other difficult behaviors.

Parenting from the Inside Out **by Daniel J. Siegel and Mary Hartzell** A rich and fascinating dive into how early childhood experiences shape the way you parent your own children. Through exercises offered in the book, parents can explore their past experiences, opening a pathway for better communication and connection with their child.

Planting Seeds: Practicing Mindfulness with Children **by Thich Nhat Hanh and the Plum Village Community** Wonderful activities, songs, and meditations for families and teachers who are interested in developing more compassion, mindfulness, and understanding in their family or classroom.

Playful Parenting **by Lawrence J. Cohen** A smart and insightful book about how play and laughter can be used to reduce conflict and build compassion and resilience in families.

Surviving and Thriving in Stepfamily Relationships: What Works and What Doesn't **by Patricia L. Papernow** Stepfamilies and practitioners alike will find this book to be an informative and useful resource that explores the challenges of stepfamilies. Using research and experiences from her clinical practice, Papernow offers suggestions of how to reduce conflict and strengthen relationships in stepfamilies.

Websites

Adobe Spark With a variety of features and graphic design templates, Adobe Spark is a good option for creating a family newsletter and other graphics.

AhaParenting.com If you have questions about parenting from pregnancy to adolescence, this is a positive parenting resource that helps parents understand how to regulate their own emotions and connect with their child.

BigLifeJournal.com This website is replete with journals, workbooks, printables, lesson plans, and other resources for parents and educators that help you implement the growth mind-set approach at home or in the classroom.

Canva.com A graphic design site that's easy and fun to use. From family newsletters to résumés and social media posts, Canva is filled with easy-to-use templates.

HandInHandParenting.org The Hand in Hand Parenting website offers a plethora of articles, audios, videos, and courses in Parenting by Connection—a positive parenting approach that helps parents and children build a strong emotional bond while managing challenging behaviors.

ParentChildConnection.com Parent Coach and author Julie Johnson works with parents of toddlers to teens, helping them develop the tools they need to turn their child's challenging behaviors around. In her blog, she shares helpful suggestions on how to handle a variety of parenting challenges and offers parent coaching services for individuals, couples, and groups.

Visme.co Create charts, graphs, social media graphics, and more with this site.

Apps

I Can Animate Compatible with Android devices, I Can Animate helps you create stop-motion animation videos with photos or drawings. No cables, other cameras, or external equipment are required.

iMotion (iOS) If you're looking to create stop-motion or time-lapse videos, this is another great option. It provides a large array of features and is easy to use.

PlantSnap With over 500,000 species in the database, this app helps you identify flowers, trees, cacti, succulents, and more. In addition, PlantSnap offers advice for growing and maintaining plants and gardens.

Stop Motion Studio Compatible with Android, iPhone, and iPad, the Stop Motion Studio App is easy to use and creates quality stop-motion animation and time-lapse films.

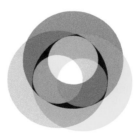

REFERENCES

Adichie, Chimamanda Ngozi. "The Danger of a Single Story." Filmed July 2009 at TEDGlobal 2009 in Oxford, UK. TED video, 19:16. YouTube.com/watch?v=D9Ihs24lzeg.

Cousins, Norman. *Anatomy of an Illness (as Perceived by the Patient)*. New York: W.W. Norton & Company, 1979.

Gordon, James S. *Transforming Trauma: The Path to Hope and Healing*. New York: HarperCollins, 2021.

INDEX

V

W

Acknowledgments

It takes a small team of committed fans to support someone in a creative endeavor, and I feel so lucky to have a family who has been just that. When I told my stepdaughter, Leyla, that I was writing a book, she said, "That's so exciting. I'll be your biggest fan!" Leyla's love, courage, and creative projects have inspired us all throughout the years.

A huge thank-you to my partner, Octavio, whose unwavering belief in me has kept me steady and afloat, even as I've had to visit my mother in the hospital on days I've also had to write. The hours we spent brainstorming and sharing ideas were invaluable.

And a million thanks to my son, Camilo, who has offered numerous unsolicited words and gestures of encouragement—a hug as I'm writing, a high five as I turned in the next milestone, and the suggestion to celebrate each step of the way.

Finally, a boatload of gratitude to my mother, who has always been my original fan. Her unflagging support, generosity, and encouragement have helped me climb mountains again and again.

About the Author

Julie Johnson has been in the field of education for over 20 years as a teacher, researcher, and parent coach. For the last 10 years, she has worked with parents who have toddlers, teens, and everything in between, helping them develop the tools they need to turn their child's challenging behaviors around.

CPSIA information can be obtained
at www.ICGtesting.com
Printed in the USA
JSHW031702291221
21636JS00004B/95